Mar

Walking the
Camino de Levante

Two women - both over 70 - walk 1,300 km
across Spain

Introduction

In April 2014, two women, both over 70, face a great challenge. Their intention is to walk the Camino de Levante. This pilgrimage route leads across Spain, from Valencia on the Mediterranean Sea to Santiago de Compostela, and on to Cap Finisterre on the Atlantic.

Who are the two women? They are

Margrit Wipf, born and raised in Zurich, and now living in Klosters (CH). She had started writing travel diaries at an early age, until now exclusively for her private use. She is the author of this book.

and

Ursula Austermann, resident in Aachen (D). She is an enthusiastic pilgrim and has already walked all the Caminos de Santiago in the meantime.

Since spring 2008, both women, independently of each other, have been walking the various St. James Ways (Caminos de Santiago) in Spain. In 2010, they meet on the Camino del Norte (Coastal Way) and walk together to Santiago de Compostela. This encounter resulted in a friendship that continues to this day.

Note: This book is not intended to be a pilgrim's guide nor a travel guide. Rather, I would like to take readers on an entertaining and exciting pilgrimage. To bring them closer to the wonderful country of Spain with many unknown areas and facets. A country that few people know in this way.

Imprint

Bibliographic information of the German National Library: The German National Library lists this publication in the German National Bibliography; detailed bibliographic data are available on the Internet at http://dnb.dnb.de.

English first edition 2022

© 2022 Margrit Wipf

Translation from German into English by Margrit Wipf partly using DeepL Pro Translator

Production and publisher: BoD - Books on Demand, Norderstedt

ISBN: 9783754351536

Recognition

I would like to thank the following persons:

Ursula Austermann that she agreed to walk the Camino de Levante with me. Alone I would never have walked this beautiful Camino. Muchas gracias.

Ruth Duppenthaler, my sister, who has been walking parts of my Caminos since 2009. It is always an enrichment to be on the road with you.

Walter Häni, a longtime friend who spontaneously offered his help to proofread my book. His love for writing, his sharp eye and his experience on pilgrimages have contributed to the good success of this work. Muchas gracias.

Theo den Otter, pilgrim friend from Holland, without his reports and videos about the Camino de Levante from 2013 I might not have dared to go this way. Many thanks.

Map Camino de Levante

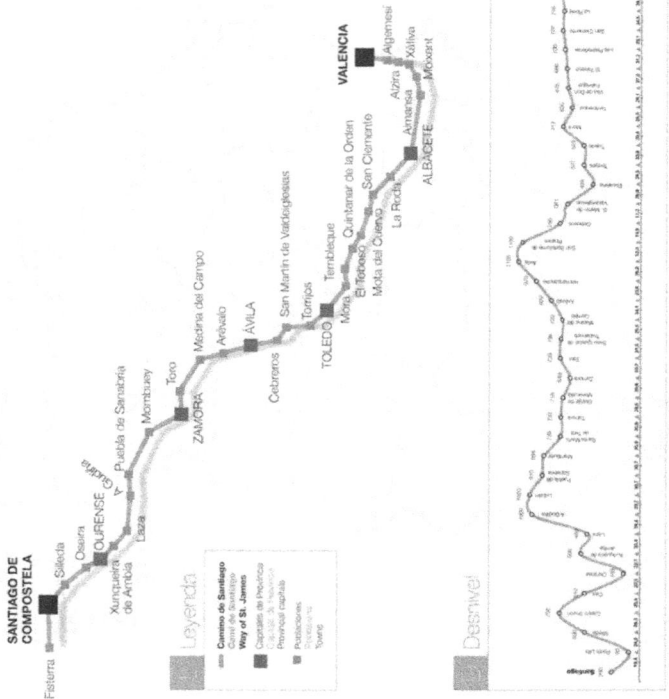

Published with permission of the Asociación Amigos del Camino de Santiago-Comunidad Valenciana, which owns the COPYRIGHT for this map.

The Camino de Levante crosses Spain from Valencia in the southeast to Santiago de Compostela in the extreme northwest and leads mostly through unknown and lonely landscapes.

At the beginning it runs through great orange and peach orchards south of Valencia and crosses La Mancha (known from the book Don Quixote de la Mancha). It passes through the world-famous cities of Toledo (UNESCO World Heritage Site), high above the Tajo River, Ávila, the highest city in Spain, Toro (with the imposing church Colegiata de Santa María la Mayor) and Zamora (the Romanesque city), located on the Duero River. Finally, the route reaches the province of Galicia and the destination of Santiago de Compostela via the Camino Sanabrés.

In fall of 2013, the desire for a new trip came up. To walk the almost unknown Way of St. James (Camino de Santiago) in spring of 2014. When I asked Ursula Austermann, a pilgrim friend from Aachen, she was immediately on fire for this ambitious project. Thereupon followed an intensive planning period. I studied the pilgrimage guide, delved into the description of the stages, consulted the maps, and rummaged through my Spain travel guide.

As always, I created a first draft for our pilgrimage. When Ursula and I compared our stage plans, we always found that we only had to make a few adjustments. Somehow, we feel the same.

Valencia, Sightseeing Day 1

Mid-April 2014. Last night I arrived in Valencia, coming from Zurich, together with Ursula. It is beautiful spring weather, and everywhere trees and flowers are blooming. In addition, there is the intensive scent of orange blossoms. In Spain they are called Azahar or Flor de Azahar. My travel diary says that Ursula wants to buy perfume or eau de toilette with this scent. However, for now, that will have to wait, as we are just at the beginning of a long pilgrimage across all of Spain.

Before we leave in 2 days, we visit the city of Valencia, which offers a wealth of sights. Beautiful Art Nouveau buildings, the cathedral and the large Mercat Central, one of the largest market halls in Europe, where vegetables, fruits, fish, meat, etc. are sold. Numerous cafes and restaurants along the streets where you can enjoy a coffee in mild spring temperatures. In the old riverbed of the Turía River there is a complex of superlatives - La Ciudad de las Artes y Ciencias, futuristic glass and concrete buildings reflected in water basins. It was designed by the world-famous architect Santiago Calatrava. Somehow 'megalomaniac' beautiful.

On a city tour we let Valencia pass us by. The old hymn to this beautiful city plays repeatedly from the headphones:

- Valencia, es la tierra de las flores de la luz y del amor
- Valencia, tus mujeres todas tienen de las rosas el color
- Valencia, al sentir como perfuma en tus huertas el aqua
- Quisiera, en la tierra valenciana mis amores encontrar

At 5 p.m. we are expected at the office of the Asociación Amigos del Camino de Santiago-Comunidad Valenciana to pick up our ordered pilgrim passports and to get the first stamp for our pilgrimage route. Afterwards, we go to the Estación Norte train station to check out the train connections for the day after next from Valencia to Silla. At the end of the day my trip meter shows 20 km again, as much as a day's stage. Back at the hotel we end the day with a wonderful paella and a glass of red wine.

Valencia, Sightseeing Day 2

Last night Ursula and I spontaneously decided on a Camino motto. It is called 'Dal Mediterráneo al Atlántico' (from the Mediterranean to the Atlantic). We go to the sandy beach near our hotel after breakfast to stand barefoot in the Mediterranean with our pants rolled up. It feels wonderful to be standing in the warm sea water at the beginning of a long walk all over Spain. Afterwards we continue sightseeing Valencia, partly by bus or then on foot.

At the beginning we go to the new marina. With the victory of the Swiss yacht Alinghi on the 31st America's Cup (2003), Switzerland suddenly rose to become an 'ocean nation'. Since we are a landlocked country, the 32nd America's Cup was held in Valencia, Spain, in 2007, and the harbor was upgraded accordingly for this major event.

Afterwards we visit the Lonja (Silk Exchange), the Ayuntamiento (City Hall) and stroll again through the Mercat Central to buy some provisions for tomorrow.

Travel Guide. Since my first Camino through Spain, I like to consult the Spain travel guides of Michael Müller Verlag for information on the country and its people. The author Thomas Schröder offers in these guides, in addition to accurately researched information, a variety of tips on accommodation and dining options.

There would still be a lot to visit in Valencia, but as always when I find myself at the beginning of a pilgrimage, my 'pilgrim heart' finally wants to go.

Pilgrim mode. Before we are back in 'pilgrim mode', here is some elementary information about the 'Caminos de Santiago' (Way of St. James) in Spain. The paths are marked with yellow arrows, with way stones or 'St. James shells'. There are several pilgrim guides for these paths. I like to use the yellow outdoor guides in German of the Conrad Stein Verlag. The route descriptions contain detailed kilometer information for the stages, information about overnight accommodations and map sections. The route is described in detail, including alternative routes. These guides are an informative support for planning your own pilgrimage route and during the Camino itself, they are also always good for the most incredible information.

Back at the hotel we pack our backpacks and have a light dinner.

PART ONE

VALENCIA - ZAMORA

1 Valencia (Silla) - Algemessí

Incredibly, today we really start!

The alarm clock wakes us up at 5:30 a.m. From our hotel we have received a picnic breakfast, which we will eat on the way. The cab to Norte station picks us up as ordered. So early in the morning there is no traffic, and we catch an earlier train from Valencia to Silla. The first stage from Valencia to Algemessí is with 37 km much too long for us and we have already decided in advance to walk only from Silla.

At 07:25 we start walking. At first, there are still some clouds on the sky and some wind, but it feels good to be on the road again. The Camino de Levante is well marked and today mostly flat. We walk through huge orange plantations. There are ripe oranges hanging from the orange trees and at the same time there are orange blossoms. By the way, do you know that Spain is by far the largest citrus producer in Europe?

The orchards alternate with vegetable fields. It's only our first day on the road today, and yet our visual receptivity is already being stretched. Artichokes, vegetable onions, rice plants? Our senses are sensitized. As a city dweller, we usually have little idea how much work is involved in cultivation, care and, later, harvesting. As we pass a large onion field, the farmer offers us one of his vegetable onions as provisions. We decline with thanks. On the way we look with interest at the numerous irrigation systems with the switching aggregates for water supply. To our surprise, the

Policia Local suddenly drives past us on the nature trail and asks us with interest about our destination. With the 'St. James shell' on the backpack, it is clear 'Santiago de Compostela'!

It is hot and I am glad that I packed a long-sleeved, breathable, shirt shortly before departure, which now protects me from the burning sun. In the pilgrimage office in Valencia, the lady had informed us that we should protect ourselves well, because the temperatures would rise to very high values in the coming days.

At 10:30 a.m. short stop for coffee in Almussafes. After that, there is no longer a place to stop. No shady spot, no bench - nada!!! Towards the end of the stage, workers pass by on their way to the lunch break, greet us and ask 'Santiago'? When we nod, they look at us admiringly. Some think they have misheard and then say 'peró no andando? ' (but not on foot?). Yes, yes, on foot. Well, we hope that we will arrive, but we don't know for sure. After all, it is 1'200 km and more than 2 months to Santiago.

As usual, the last hour drags on. At 2:30 p.m. we finally arrive in Algemessí and look first for a restaurant for lunch. After having eaten, we immediately feel better.

At the town hall, where the Policia Local is located, we show our pilgrim passport and identity card. The pilgrim's passport is also the authorization for the use of the official Albergue de Peregrinos (pilgrim's hostel). The copy of the identity card is used by the police for statistical purposes.

We thought that we would not meet any other pilgrims, but wrong! Stephane, a young Belgian guy is already there and later a younger German couple arrives. We only see the woman; her partner is injured, and the police drive them both to the hospital. Later, an older German says, he would like to join us, but we do not want to.

2 Algemessí - Xàtiva

The night was restless with much noise from the street. At 11 p.m. the German pilgrims returned from the hospital. The man injured his shoulder badly and cannot continue the Camino. They have no choice but to fly back home after the first day. It is bad when you must stop a Camino for health reasons, but already after the first day!!!

Our alarm clock goes off at 05:45 a.m. Quietly we dress, stow the remaining utensils in the backpack and after a short morning toilet we go out of the house. Again, this stage would be 29 km long. In order not to overstress our body already at the beginning, we take the train for the first part of the way to Carcaixent. Departure at 06.20 o'clock. By train it takes only 7 min, on foot we would have needed 2 ½ hours for the 9.6 km. Arrived in Carcaixent we look for a bar for breakfast. On the way there is one open. Unfortunately, there is no real breakfast, but at least a coffee and some 'Magdalenas' (pastries). Off we go at 07:30.

Today, our way leads again through huge orange and peach plantations. Past a reed belt teeming with mosquitoes, and past fields of artichokes and vegetables. Soon, the landscape becomes more varied, and a mountain range can be seen on the horizon. Our destination is Xàtiva (also spelled Játiva), the city of the popes. Two later appointed popes were born here, Pope Calixtinus III and Pope Alexander VI.

Arriving in Xàtiva, we are really 'deshechas' (exhausted). The body screams 'thirst, hunger, shade' and only wants a place to sit down and rest. So as usual, we immediately look for a place to have lunch. After that, the spirits of life come back quickly.

Afterwards we go to our booked accommodation. I am physically still a bit tired, but ok. Later in the afternoon we go down to the city. After an extensive sightseeing incl. church, papal statues, buildings etc. we sit down outside on a pretty plaza and have a Copita (means 'little glass'). We use this term on our Caminos as a general term for an aperitif.

Pilgrimage

What fascinates us about this ancient form of being on the road? And why do hundreds of thousands of people of all ages and nationalities take this risk every year? I will write about this topic later in this book.

In addition to the desire on walking through a foreign country, I certainly have a bit of a pioneering spirit. In my mind I often ask myself, what's around the next bend? And if I then stand on a crossing, which opens the view over a beautiful new landscape, my body releases endorphins. Is that how happiness is defined?

Everyday pilgrimage

Anyone who has ever been on a pilgrimage route, knows that the daily stages usually follow a pattern. Our stages are about 20 km long and our daily routine in Spain looks like this:

The alarm is set for 6 o'clock a.m., getting up, morning toilet, finishing packing the backpack and go to breakfast at 06:30. In the rural areas there is usually an open bar, where you can get a coffee and a dry pastry. In southern regions our favorite breakfast is 'Pan tostado con aceite y tomate y ajo' (toasted bread slices, olive oil, freshly chopped tomatoes and garlic). And let's not forget, the freshly squeezed orange jus. Delicious!

Provided it already has fresh bread, we change our routine and order a 'bocadillo' (sandwich) with cheese or 'jamón serrano' (dried ham). We then eat half for breakfast and have the other half packed as sandwich.

We start walking in the morning around 07:00 a.m. Depending on the temperatures, it can also be shortly after sunrise. The cool morning hours are perfect for hiking. It is not hot yet; the light has a pastel coloring, and all birds are singing (spring is mating season after all).

We walk, lost in our thoughts. Meditative walking alternates with enthusiastic exclamations or silent wonder. Between 9 and 10 o'clock we take a break. If there is a place with an open bar along, we stop in. We order coffee or water and eat our sandwich. Afterwards we continue and between 1 and 2 p.m. we usually arrive at the stage place.

During our various Caminos de Santiago, we have adapted our eating habits. In the first years, like most pilgrims, I carried some bread and cheese for a sandwich, and in the evening, I had a hard time finding an open restaurant. The Spaniards eat very late, that is, after 9 p.m. or even later. As a pilgrim, you want to go to bed early and besides, the pilgrim hostels close at 10 pm. On top of that, I don't sleep well with a full stomach.

In 2010, my sister Ruth and I arrived at a stage location way too early, and the pilgrim's hostel didn't open until 3 p.m. Spontaneously, we decided to have lunch at a restaurant nearby. We were impressed by the quality and variety of the daily menu.

Here is an example of a daily menu, also called pilgrim menu in regions with many pilgrims.
As first course there is 'Ensalada mista' (mixed salad), soup, egg dish, 'Lentejas' (lentils with 'Chorizo' (paprika sausage), or 'Garbanzos' (chickpea stew).
The main course consists of meat, chicken, or fish, prepared in a variety of ways and is usually served with potatoes.
For 'postre' (dessert) you can choose from cake, flan, fruit, and yogurt.

The price of about 9 € includes water and wine, and the portions are always generous. Since we found out about the daily menu, we have lunch in a restaurant with the 'Menu del Día' (menu of the day) and eat only a yogurt and some fruit in the evening.

After lunch we go to our accommodation. This can be a B&B, a hotel, or a pilgrim hostel, depending on availability. I first go to sleep for an hour. Followed then by showers, washing, hanging laundry, and writing my diary. For the diary, I spend about an hour per day.

Spain still has 'siesta' from about 2 p.m. to 5pm. This means that nothing is open before 5 p.m. Here, too, a routine has crept in with us. Shopping for the evening and for the following leg. Water, Aquarius (a drink that replaces the lost minerals to the body), a fruit, (orange, apple, apricots, or cherries) and yogurt.

In spring, Spain offers the sweetest oranges I've ever tasted. Although an apple is easier to eat while walking, I always buy oranges. Towards mid of June, they become drier and don't taste as good anymore. Time for cherries and apricots arrives.

After that, another highlight is coming up for us. Sitting comfortably on a plaza and talking about the beautiful day with a glass of Verdejo (Spanish white wine). We discuss tomorrow's stage, look for the way out of town, look for a bar for breakfast and visit one or two sights. On these tours we always walk another 5 km.

Back in our accommodation, we bring in the dry laundry, eat something small, and pack the backpack for tomorrow. Satisfied with our day of pilgrimage, we go to bed around 10 pm.

3 Xátiva - Moixent

Even though I sometimes feel tired and exhausted after a day's stage, on the following day this is blown away.

Yesterday evening we were too tired to climb up to the castle of Xátiva and postponed the visit to this morning. Somehow, such views make me satisfied. I look down on the land, that we have been walking through, and I feel proud of what we have achieved.

The first two stages were mostly flat, but now, the path slowly begins to climb. Partially it is only 100 meters of altitude per day, but with the days, the altitude adds up and in Almansa we shall already be at 700 m above sea level.

The path is varied. We walk through almond orchards and past the first broom bushes. Because of the visit to the Castillo of Xátiva, we only left at 10 o'clock. For this reason, we decided to eat in Canals, a village in middle of the stage, and thus arrived in Moixent only around 5 p.m.

In this place we spend the night in the Red Cross house of the municipality. First, we go to the Policia Local, get registered and get the key to the Cruz Roja cottage. It is small, has 2 bunk beds, has a shower and a toilet. Of course, such accommodations cannot be compared with usual hostels or hotel rooms. These are simple emergency accommodations that the communities along the way provide for the pilgrims.

4 Moixent - La Font de la Figuera

In the pilgrim's guidebook Camino de Levante, there are notes, that on most stages there are no places to stop during the day. This means that you must carry enough water with you.

In addition to the almond and olive trees, the vineyards show up. During the next 10 km, the path winds along the hills and offers again and again beautiful views down into the river valley. In the newspaper 'El Levante' of Saturday we read that the current drought in the Comunidad Valenciana (Valencian Region) would ruin the harvest. To our amazement we see that earth has been piled up around the trunks of the olive trees, probably to preserve the moisture.

At km 11 there is a very nice property. A sign indicates 'Mas de Monserrat'. The guidebook says that you can get coffee and homemade cakes there. Although it is a detour of 10 min, we go there anyway. The Casa Rural (country house) is very nice but has no more restaurant service. The owner offers us a tea anyway and shows us the house. The rooms are nicely decorated, in typical country style. Unfortunately, we cannot stay for long, so that turns out to be a short visit. What follows now, is a nice stretch of path, partly in shade of a grove, and finally we come to the 3 oak trees described in the guidebook with a place to sit in the shade. Que lujo!

In La Font de la Figuera we spend the night in the pilgrim's cottage next to the sports field. Nearby is one of the longest lavaderos (public laundry house) in Spain. The lavadero is no longer used and we are the only women who do their laundry here.

5 La Font de la Figuera - Almansa

This will be the longest stage for us since Valencia. According to the guide it is almost 30 km long. We start walking already at 06.40. It's still gloomy, but we looked closely at the start of the stage last night so as not to go wrong. The sunrise will be only at 07.20. After some time, the trail passes through a 'hare country'. I have never seen so many hares in the wild. Further the trail goes through a canyon, and it smells wonderful of Mediterranean pine forests. Besides the many hares, there are also large birds, yet unknown to us, and we hear the first cuckoo on this Camino.

Unfortunately, this beautiful part of the stage is soon over. What follows is a monotonous long stretch, along a car road and a railroad track. The sun burns down on us, and we absolutely dislike this stretch. In distance we can see the defiant castle of Almansa, but it is still very, very, far away. We arrive in town at the last minute. Because the helpful yellow arrows or shells are missing, we must ask several times for a restaurant. Near the city park there is a bar, but it only offers 'Plato Combinado' (plate dish). Although it is not a menu of the day, the food tastes excellent. 'Verdura a la plancha' (grilled vegetables), 2 'huevos fritos' (fried eggs) and patatas fritas. Muy rico, delicious.

At home on maps

In my travel notes I often write about landscapes, areas, 'sierras' (mountain ranges) as if they were laid out before me. In fact, from an early age I developed a great interest in geography and topography. I looked at maps, at the atlas and searched for countries, rivers, and mountains.

Over the years I have realized that I have a kind of visual imagination of areas that I will walk through in future. I also have a strong memory for the topography of areas I have walked through.

During my planning for a Camino, I can visualize the whole path spread out in front of me, as if marked on a map.

To my great delightment, Reise Know-How (producer of travel maps) has started to produce maps in size 1:350 000, tear and water resistant, very good readability, and printed on both sides. Such a map is always in my backpack. Of course, I can look at the information on the iPhone, on map APPs, on or offline, but for larger areas I still like to consult a good map.

6 Almansa - Alpera

As usual, we start walking very early. After half an hour I turn around and am speechless. It looks fantastic, Almansa in the morning haze!!! Mystical like a painting from earlier times. Emotionally this is pure happiness, in contrast to our arrival yesterday.

The trail follows the left flank of the Sierra del Mudrón. A barren, but fascinating area. Again and again, rabbits scamper through the fields. We cross many private properties, which are labeled with the signs 'Prohibido el paso, zona particular'. But pilgrims have right of way, and we must only close the gates again. After 3 hours we reach the only tree in this vast landscape and eat our sandwich in its shade.

Yesterday we reached the autonomous region of Castilla-La Mancha. In front of us is a landscape (La Mancha), that we have been looking forward to for a long time, but only now that we are here, we really can sense and absorb it.

Today's stage is extraordinary. We are by far the only people in this grandiose expanse. The stage to Higueruela would be about 40 km long and so we follow a detour on the Ruta de la Lana to Alpera. Towards 1 p.m. we arrive at Alpera, a small little village, check in at our hostel and go directly for lunch.

My body is slowly getting accustomed to the daily walks, but after lunch I always look forward to the Siesta. I find it very relaxing to rest or sleep for an hour, while the heat shimmers outside.

7 Alpera - Higueruela

Today's stage leads along a lightly traveled side road. Silencio absoluto! Only the birds in the cornfields can be heard. Their chirping is so beautiful and loud. What kind of birds might they be? In meantime, I learned that they are skylarks. They have their nests in cornfields and raise their brood in nests on the ground. By the time the corn is ready for harvest, the young birds are already fledged, and all are gone.

The path climbs leisurely and the higher we get, the wider is the panoramic view over the surrounding landscape. Due to the altitude (900 meters above sea level), the vegetation has also changed, and it now smells intensely of rosemary and thyme. Towards the end of the stage, we cross a hill and suddenly, we see the village of Higueruela with its many windmills in front of us. This village situated at 1'039 meters above sea level is the highest place on the way so far. A very well-kept place with free Wi-Fi for everyone.

We spend the night in a nice hotel in the village. Later in the afternoon, two Spaniards arrive with bikes, who will spend the night in the hostel. Later, a young German pilgrim arrives, who has walked the whole route from Almansa. Apparently, she felt fine at the turnoff to Alpera, but overdid it and later suffered a lot from the heat and sun. When she arrived, she was dehydrated and sunburned. Fortunately, we always start early in the morning and also protect our skin with high density sun blocker.

8 Hoya Gonzalo - Chinchilla de Monte Aragón

The bus from Higueruela to Hoya Gonzalo leaves around 07 a.m. If you are interested to know, how the bus system in Spain works? Switzerland is known for having public transport (train and bus) arriving and departing on the minute. But Spain doesn't have to hide with its bus and train system either. Since 2008, I have been traveling to different areas in Spain and I know in meantime that the country is very well connected with public transport. The bus routes can be found online, and you only must be at the bus stop at the specified time.

The temperature has become a little more bearable. In addition, there is also a little wind blowing and it is a pleasant walk. The colors of the landscape are amazing, I had little imagination of how beautiful this would be.

Sometime between 10 and 11 o'clock, the bikers from yesterday overtake us. They are surprised to meet us already so far ahead. We explain them the bus possibility because we do not want to walk 30 km. For these 'chicos' (young men) that makes absolute sense.

Today we are also spoiled with beautiful picnic spots. There are always big stones to sit on along the way. After 1 p.m. we are already in Chinchilla de Monte Aragón. This place is located on a mountain, and we shall visit the castle, overlooking the village in late afternoon. The air is very clear, and we can already see the city of Albacete in the distance.

9 Chinchilla de Monte Aragón - Albacete

The day begins with cold fingers. It is only 6° and at this moment I decide not to send the warm fleece jacket home after all. We start at 06:40 and the sky shows itself in delicate pastel colors.

After a short time, we are all alone on the path and merge completely with nature.

It remains cool and I keep my long-sleeved shirt on during the whole stage. Shortly after 10 o'clock we already reach the Parador of Albacete, located outside the city, and decide spontaneously to stop for a coffee. The cafeteria is still closed, and we are asked into the dining room, where the guests of the Paradores are sitting at the late breakfast. We are marveled at and when a guest sees our backpacks with the 'St. James 'St. James shell', he comes to our table and asks, if we are pilgrims of St. James. "Yes, we started in Valencia and by now, have walked 200 km and still have another 1,000 km to go".

From the Parador there is only a 6 km walk to the city. We feel very fit on arrival, we could easily have walked another 10 km. But today Albacete is our stage destination and we have planned a rest day here for tomorrow.

10 Albacete, Sunday, and rest day

At 6 o'clock we are already awake, but do not get up yet. Promptly we fall asleep again and wake up 08:30 for the second time. For breakfast we go outside. We are surprised that all bars are still closed. Finally, we find an open bar/pastry shop behind the cathedral, called La Suíza. Apparently, a compatriot of mine has settled here. Although today is Sunday, a department store outside the city is open. I must buy rubber plugs for my telescopic sticks, somehow, I can't find them anymore and the clattering on the few streets disturbs me.

One day off every 10 to 14 days is recommended in order not the overwork the body, so to keep the physical balance at its best.

In a 'Locutorio' (internet store) I write my first Camino email to friends and readers of my 'Camino Mails'. Ursula reads the Sunday newspaper El País.

Afterwards we go for sightseeing and later have some lunch. As usual, while Ursula strolls around the city, I lie down for a siesta nap. Later we meet and study the stages for the coming days.

Autonomous Communities and Provinces

Since the territorial reform carried out in 1833, Spain has been divided into 17 Autonomous Communities (Comunidades Autónomas). The additional division into provinces remained the basis of Spain's territorial division until the adoption of the new Spanish Constitution of 1978.

For most tourists, and for me, the differentiation between province and autonomous region was not always clear at the beginning of my pilgrimages. On the Camino Francés, the most traveled pilgrimage route, after crossing the Pyrenees, the trails lead into the province of Navarra. Navarra is one of the exceptions where the province is also the Autonomous Region.

On the Camino de Levante we shall walk through five Autonomous Communities (also called regions) and many provinces. The first is the Comunidad Valenciana, then it leads through Castilla-La Mancha. Almost unnoticed, the trail then passes through the southeastern part of the Region of Madrid for one day. This is followed by long kilometers and days in which we will be in Castilla y León, before finally crossing the region of Galicia.

Since Almansa we are in Castilla-La Mancha and only by now, I feel to have arrived in la Mancha. In this endless vast area, without hills or mountains, in middle of huge fields of grain, some of which are lined with cornflowers and poppies. Vineyards reaching to the horizon, alternating with peach orchards, almond and olive groves, or garlic fields.

11 Albacete - La Gineta

For the next 10 days we will walk mostly on flat terrain. Let's see how we like it.

In Spain, all restaurants and bars have large TV screens that show the latest information and weather forecasts from early in the morning until late at night. For the next 2 weeks the weather will remain the same, i.e., sun, heat, and daily rising temperatures. For us, this means that we must start walking even earlier.

Out of Albacete the route choice is clear. Cross the railroad bridge and then follow the only dirt road. Here the yellow arrows are sparse and sometimes missing altogether. This is especially annoying when the path divides and the supposed main path later turns out to be wrong. When such ambiguities occur, Ursula and I look for the solution together. We look in which direction we would have to go, consult the pilgrim's guide, the map in the iPhone and let our sense of direction prevail. Sometimes I photograph such places and mark the description in the book. Depending on how problematic the spot was, I later send the information to Conrad Stein Verlag so that this can be noted in the updates.

Just before the village La Gineta, we see the church tower of the village on the left, but a busy Autovia separates us from the village and once again the arrows are missing. Fortunately, the book says to turn right and then go through an underpass to get to the other side of the highway. We are always glad for such exact indications.

In La Gineta, we first go to the Ayuntamiento (town hall) to register with the Policia Local and get the information for the accommodation. The only accommodation is in a large sports center (Centro Poli Deportivo), just outside the village. The policeman drives us there, gives us a key for the facility and shows us the location. We can spend the night in the women's dressing room on gym mats.

Afterwards he drives us back in his car and shows us a restaurant for lunch. At lunch I feel so tired that I could easily fall asleep. Ursula is also tired, but unlike me, she can still eat vigorously.

Sleeping on mats? For young people, of course, that's no big problem. If I'm tired, I can sleep anywhere. But with age that's no longer easy. I usually practice in advance at home how to sit down and getting up from the floor.

12 La Gineta - La Roda

Again, we get up at 06 o'clock. The night was not really relaxing. As already mentioned, I no longer sleep as well on the floor as in a bed. Our bar from yesterday is already open at 06.30 and so we come to our beloved breakfast 'Tostada con aceite y tomate'. With coffee and a sandwich to go, we only pay 3.50 € Incredible!

After 07 o'clock we start walking. First, we cross some road junctions, a highway traffic circle and soon we are on a sandy gravel road. In some distance, we can see the A-31 highway and the Madrid-Valencia railroad line, whose muffled roar tells us that we are not all alone in the world.

But soon we are back in the absolute silence of nature. Beautiful paths, rabbits, and warbling skylarks. On both sides of the dirt road there are some holm oaks, some with the typical gnarled rootstocks. Otherwise, grain fields and vineyards are our companions. In the middle of the stage, we cross a canal. A sign indicates that swimming in the canal is not allowed. In spring of 2013, Theo, a pilgrim I know from Holland, walked this trail. In his video there is this sign, but the canal had no water at that time!

After about 15 km the church tower of La Roda can already be seen. Around noon the heat starts to press heavily. In the shade of a large almond tree, we drink our remaining water, in order not to arrive dehydrated in the village.

On the street, an employee of the town hall talks to us and shows us the way to the restaurant 'Flor de la Mancha', where we get a sumptuous Menu del Dia (daily menu) with 2€ reduction for pilgrims.

The pilgrim accommodation in La Roda is in the sanitary room of the 'Plaza de Toros' (bullring) and it is a cozy 2-bed room with shower/WC. The hospitalero (hostel father) hands us the key for our room and gives us information about the place and the Plaza de Toros.

The church tower of La Roda is called 'El Pharo de la Mancha' (Lighthouse of La Mancha) because it can be seen from afar from all directions.

After our siesta, two Austrian pilgrims arrive. One stage behind us, a group of 5 pilgrims (three Italians, one Spaniard and one Frenchman) is on the way and because there is only room for 5 people in La Gineta, the two Austrians have skipped the stage and have come here by bus.
Suddenly other pilgrims!! Now we are no longer alone on the road.

13 La Roda - Minaya

Today, the alarm clock is set for 05:15. The bar at the Hostal Molina opens already at 06:00 and so we leave the Albergue at 05:50. The sky is very clear, and we can see millions of stars. We have never left our accommodation that early. In front of the Hotel Molina, the first guest is already waiting and then the door opens punctually. For breakfast we have a coffee and a roll. At 06.40 we start our walk. The lights of the Lighthouse are still on, it feels like being on a coast. The lights will go out only at 07.30.

An hour ago, it was starry, but now clouds show up for the first time. I think to myself that the sun will burn them later. Wrong thought. It remains all day muggy and overcast, but for walking, this feels perfect. The stage is 18 km long and with an average pace of 4 km per hour, we would arrive within 4.30 hours at the stage place We are but already in 04.20 hours there, including 20 minutes break. Easy walking!

In Minaya, the pilgrim accommodation would be again in a 'Poli Deportivo'. But since we have already reached the village at 11 o'clock, we decide for the Hostal Antolin. When we arrive that early at a stage place, we like to check-in at once and enjoy having some more time for daily duties. We then unpack our backpacks completely and possibly do some large laundry.

After 1 p.m. we usually go to have lunch. In my diary I don't mention the food, even though it was certainly tasty, but I do mention the house wine. Water and regional wine are always served with the daily menu. The quality of this wine here in Minaya really amazed me. After many years on the Caminos, I am relatively familiar with Spanish wines, but this one I found stunning. When I inquire about the wine with the owner (the bottles usually have no labels), he sends his son to describe his wine to me.

His son has studied enology and yet takes care of the family winery. He is of course delighted with the compliment and explains to us that the La Mancha winegrowers, in contrast to earlier years, produce and market their wines themselves today. Once back home, I might look out for wines of La Mancha.

Yesterday afternoon I wrote in my travel diary about the dogs on the Caminos de Santiago.

Every morning, the paths lead out of the villages, mostly past houses, and farms. These are guarded by dogs, but they are inside the fence. As soon as pilgrims arrive, they run wildly yapping along the fence. Barking at pilgrims is apparently fun for them and it maybe it's part of their morning training of the otherwise so boring daily routine.

14 Minaya - San Clemente

The morning is still gloomy. There are many clouds in the sky and a cool wind is blowing. Instead of my Krüger shirt I put on the fleece jacket. After having breakfast at the hostal, we start our stage in the twilight. It is again a pleasant walk. We often pass chozos, which are egg-shaped stone structures that used to serve as shelters for farm workers and shepherds. Once again, we cross an empty highway. For Ursula this is always a special photo subject, as a comparison to the busy highways in Germany.

To our delight we come t a village with an open bar. A rarity during the last days. The beautiful trail then follows for many kilometers with dreamlike experiences. Huge garlic fields with buds, I have never seen that before. In order to know what kind of vegetable it really is, I sometimes step into the field, and take a closer look at the plants. No doubt, this one is garlic.

Meditative walking. Sometimes it happens to me that I am lost in thoughts and walk past something very beautiful. Suddenly my brain switches to 'recording mode' and depending on what I have seen, I even go back to take a photo. In this case it was a poppy road in the cornfield.

Thanks to the pine forests, we are spoiled with shady passages today. At the end of the stage, beautiful purple flowers line the roadside, obviously a species of orchids.

We walk at a good pace and arrive at San Clemente before noon. Again, we decide to spend the night at a hostal. This place has an extremely appealing center with a beautiful

Plaza Mayor (main square), a Santiago church, and a 'Torre Vieja' (ancient tower) which we will of course climb later.

Suddenly we see other pilgrims. On the plaza sit three Italians, the two Austrians we know from La Roda and a Spaniard. In the evening I go briefly to the municipal library to clarify the booking possibility regarding the El Greco exhibition in Toledo.

Upon returning to the Hostal, André, a pilgrim from Toulouse, approaches me and we sit down together for a glass of wine. Like most pilgrims on the Camino de Levante, he has walked all the great Caminos de Santiago and knows the customs of pilgrimage life. When a pilgrim is on a pilgrimage route, they spontaneously sit down at the table with other pilgrims and immediately find a common bond.

15 San Clemente - Las Pedroñeras

Due to the weather warning for very high temperatures, the owner of the Hostal has provided for us a thermos jug with coffee. André is also up at 06 o'clock, but he shall leave later. The way out of the village is simple and easy to walk. 18°C (64°F) in early morning suggest a hot day. Behind us the sun rises and the whole sky glows in most beautiful orange color shades.

A few hours later, we see a group of pilgrims behind us. They are walking at a fast pace. We are having our drinking break and let them pass. Only André 'shifts down a gear' and decides to walk with us. As we are continuing, we see at once a large poppy field. He asks, what these flowers are called in Spanish. Without having agreed, Ursula and I sing the well-known Spanish song 'Amapola'.

- Amapola, lindísima amapola,
- Será siempre mi alma tuya sola.
- Yo te quiero, amada niña mía,
- Igual que ama la flor la luz del día.
- Amapola, lindísima amapola,
  No seas tan ingrata y ámame.
- Amapola, amapola,
  Cómo puedes tú vivir tan sola?

Continuing our way, we see a sign in a vineyard with the text 'Prohibido cazar riego'. We don't know the word 'riego', so I look it up in my translation App. 'Riego' means irrigation and text translates as 'it is forbidden to hunt the irrigation'? Somehow this doesn't make sense.

A little later we meet the owner and ask him the meaning of that sign. Because he has put an irrigation system for his vines and the water hoses are in the ground, hunting is not allowed here. All right and again learned something.

He then offers us a glass of his own wine however, considering the high temperatures we must decline.

The trail is again very interesting. We see many hares and skylarks. Then there are also those big birds that have already scared us already sometimes. André explains to us that they are pheasants.

The pheasant or partridge story tells itself like this: I'm walking, lost in thoughts, and suddenly I'm startled by a loud rattling sound coming from the nearby bushes. I scream out loud! Then, right next to the path, two large birds rise and fly away loudly protesting. I start laughing and ask myself, who has been more frightened? The birds or me?

Around 11:30 a.m. we arrive at the Castillo located near the riverbanks of Río Zancara. This imposing castle is abandoned and yet inhabited only by crows.

Soon we see our next stage town in distance. Las Pedroñeras. But it will take another 2 hours until we arrive in the 'capital of garlic'. The place has little to offer, except big garlic braids, but we can't buy them for weight reasons. Today we are not the only Santiago pilgrims at the hotel. A couple from Sweden and André are also staying here.

16 Las Pedroñeras - Mota del Cuervo

For the first time on this Camino, there are 5 pilgrims having breakfast. At 07:30 Ursula and I start walking. Today's stage, or rather today's stage place, is special. Mota del Cuervo is well known for the windmills. More about this later.

First the way follows about 2 km the Carretera (country road). Large billboards advertise the famous cheese 'Queso Manchego' (Manchego cheese).

The sheep, which graze in the pastures of central Spain, provide the basis for this semi-hard cheese with a lightly sweet aroma. The balanced flavor of Manchego ranges from sour-fruity and nutty to spicy-piquant.

The most common varieties are: Curado, a semi-hard cheese, aged between three and six months. Semicurado, a semi-hard cheese, aged between three weeks and three months and tastes slightly milder than Curado.

At the beginning, André walks a bit with us. We pass a piece of land where many hares bounce around in the early morning light. The path continues through fields, vineyards, and olive groves. When we meet a group of cyclists, we realize that today is Saturday. In Spain, many cyclists are on their training round on Saturday morning on the roads that we also use.

The road winds towards a hill and on top is a huge billboard with the 'Toro' (bull), of the brandy 'Veterano Osborne'. When I was traveling by car in Spain in the late 60's, these big billboards meant for me always the beginning of summer vacations.

After some kilometers we pass a small village, but don't stop. Further the trail continues over hills, past a large flock of sheep and around 11 o'clock we arrive at Santa Maria de los Llanos. Perfect timing for a coffee stop. Ursula and I sit on the terrace in the shade, the Swedes and André are inside. Then Ursula and I walk on. The heat is oppressive and there is little wind. After what feels like an eternity, we finally see them. The world famous seven windmills of Mota del Cuervo. We have been waiting for this view for a long time. We will spend the night in Mota del Cuervo and visit the windmills later in the afternoon.

Windmills of Mota del Cuervo.
On a small chain of hills stand seven windmills. In 1967, the town was given the name 'Balcony of La Mancha'. This because of the wide horizon that can be seen from the Molinos. Miguel de Cervantes immortalized them in his famous work 'Dcn Quixote de la Mancha'. Thus, they have become emblematic of these flat lands of La Mancha. Three of the seven mills can still be visited.

17 Mota del Cuervo - El Toboso, Sunday, ½ day of rest.

Sunrise and views back to the Molinos. The dirt road leads over hills and past beautifully tended vineyards. On the driveway of a winery there are large terracotta water tanks in which we would easily fit in. Break at a nice rest area just before El Toboso. Then, accompanied by the sound of church bells, we walk through an avenue of intensely smelling trees to the village. Later we asked at the information about the trees, it is Persian lilac.

El Toboso is a small village with a beautiful Plaza Mayor. This place became famous through Miguel de Cervantes novel 'Don Quixote de La Mancha'. Those who have read this book remember his fight against the windmills, giants in his eyes, or Dulcinea's transformation from a simple peasant girl into a noble lady.

Unfortunately, at 10 o'clock everything is still closed. So, we go to the Hostal/Albergue El Quijote mentioned in the pilgrimage guide and get a coffee with pastries there. We can soon move into our room and then visit the village with the Don Quijote Museum. For lunch we go back to our hostal. Washing, siesta, writing, and more sightseeing in the village. In meantime, two more pilgrims (mother and daughter from Holland) have arrived. They are on their way to Santiago de Compostela with two horses.

18 El Toboso - La Villa de Don Fadrique

Yesterday evening we discussed the division of the stage, because 26.8 km are really exhausting in this heat. We had decided to drive a part of the way by bus today.

The early morning is cool and there is a strong wind. Nevertheless, it is a beautiful walk through gently undulating vineyards. The Spanish would say 'una madrugada maravillosa', a beautiful morning atmosphere. And these times also give beautiful pictures. We walk briskly and reach already around 08.30 Quintana de la Orden. From here we wanted to get the 09:00 bus, but Ursula only has coffee on her mind. Breakfast or bus? Since one never knows if we would get breakfast later, we decide for breakfast and promptly miss the bus. Afterwards we walk along the country road for 5 km. The landscape is flat and dry, but there are vineyards on all sides to the horizon. At 11:30 we arrive Puebla de Almoradiel. From here it is another 9 km to the next stage destination. Another 2 ½ hours in this heat; I decide to go by bus. Ursula wants to walk. The bus left earlier than indicated (yes, that also exists) and so I walk back to the bar to ask for a cab. An acquaintance of the landlady offers to take me to La Villa de Don Fadrique, since he must bring his daughter there anyway. I accept with thanks. Flat, shimmering heat and very landscape. I am glad that I did not walk this piece.

In La Villa de Don Fadrique we will once again spend the night in the Sports Center. The two pilgrims with their horses will also spend the night here. From them we learn how exhausting such a pilgrimage with horses is. When we two arrive at the stage destination we can make ourselves comfortable. But first, they must take care of the horses. This is a lot of work and requires precise planning.

At 5:30 p.m. it is still very hot!

La Villa de Don Fadrique - Toledo
The next three days will be dedicated to a great stage.
Toledo, UNESCO World Heritage Site, capital of Castilla-La-Mancha and 3 days stay.
A round birthday and a visit from Switzerland. But first we must walk the remaining three days.

19 La Villa de Don Fadrique (Villacañas) - Tembleque

This stage is with 29 km again too long for us and therefore we drive with the morning bus to Villacañas. At 7 o'clock we are already there and look for a breakfast shop. Even if the place seems to be deserted, there is always someone you can ask. In our case it is a man bent over the trunk of his car. There is a simple bar close by and we get the best fresh sliced tomatoes to go with our tostada. Another sandwich to go and off we go. First 2 km on the country road until we get out of town. Then on dirt roads past vineyards, cornfields with bright blue cornflowers and olive groves. To the right, the Sierra Romeral Mountain range can be seen. The path climbs slowly, allowing views over the open country.

Then, the path follows a pine forest and passes through well-tended olive plantations. After a break in an olive grove, we cross hills again and slowly see in which direction Tembleque lies. Soon we can see the church tower and the windmills in the distance. At 1 p.m. we arrive.

Everything is close together. Church, restaurant and a nice Casa Rural where we will spend the night. Tembleque is known for its beautiful marketplace, which we will visit later in the afternoon. Ingrid and Eva, the pilgrims with the horses, spend the night at the same place, and later we meet a French couple who will also walk all the way to Santiago.

20 Tembleque - Mora

The pilgrims guide says that there is no village to stop on the way. The stage is 3-part. First, the trail leads through flat grain fields. In contrast to the past weeks, the grain here will soon be ready for harvesting.

I have been walking in Spain for years and I have seen a lot of cereals in various stages of growth. Unlike Ursula, who knows all the cereals, I can identify with certainty only oats. Again and again, I plan to delve into the subject of cereals on the Internet after my return. Unfortunately, it always remains with the attempt. In meantime, I know that Spain is one of the world's largest producers of oats (3rd), barley (5th), rye (8th) and wheat (19th). In addition, many legumes are grown here, such as chickpeas and lentils.

After the cornfields along stretch through a surreal karst landscape follows and finally olive plantations stretch to the horizon. A strenuous stage. There are only a few lines in my travel diary today. Apparently, the stage was really exhausting. On my photos I can see in retrospect the difficulty of the stage. Again and again, I can see how our path resembles a plowed field and we must go through it. And that for over 25 km!

21 Mora (Nambroca) - Toledo

The stage from Mora to Toledo is 39 km long and without accommodations on the way. Therefore, we stand early morning at the bus station and wait for the bus to Nambroca, which is situated in half of the stage. Once there we find the yellow arrow immediately and start walking.

There are two options for this route. Option A – lonely trail through wild romantic terrain with partly magnificent views over olive plantations, but without a village. Option B - through a village with bar, but without beautiful views. We decide for the variant A.

It is again a beautiful trail, which leads on small side roads or through olive groves and shady little valleys. We are full of anticipation for Toledo. Around 11:30 we arrive at the rest area that is described in the outdoor guide, from where you can already see Toledo, 3 km away. A short rest and then we move on. We pass a small Ermita before reaching the panoramic road. The view of the city of Toledo is overwhelming. The whole city lies before us as if on a platter. Only the deep Tajo gorge separates us from the city. At a nice viewpoint with a bar, we stop to celebrate our arrival with glass of cool white wine and some tapas.

But we are not quite there yet.

First, we continue to the Alcántara Bridge, cross this historic bridge, and then climb the many steps to the main square of Toledo, the 'Plaza de Zocodover'.

After almost three weeks on lonely roads and in mostly small towns, we suddenly find ourselves in a big city, surrounded by thousands of tourists.

We make our way through the narrow streets of the old town to the Jewish Quarter (Judería), where our booked hotel 'Pintor El Greco' is located. In the preparation phase for this pilgrimage, I had already planned our stay here in Toledo many months in advance. In the Spain travel guide of the Michael Müller publishing house, there was a tip of the author Thomas Schröder for the hotel 'Pintor El Greco'. A typical Toledan house of the 17th century, which is one of the most beautiful hotels in Toledo. I followed his tip and booked the rooms for us. Arrived in Toledo, what a feeling! 3 ½ weeks on foot, 480 km walked, safe and sound – incredible!

Some of the pilgrims we met along the way are only going as far as Toledo. They don't have that much time this year and plan to come back here in next years to continue their journey. We feel privileged of being able to continue our pilgrimage. Beautiful!

But first, we will stay here for three nights, visit this beautiful city and I am also expecting the arrival of my sister Ruth from Zurich tomorrow.

22 Friday, May 16, my 70th birthday

Since I set out on my first Camino de Santiago in spring of 2008, I've gotten used to always celebrate my birthday somewhere along the way in Spain.

This year, however, it is not just anywhere on the road. Since spring 2009, my sister Ruth always walks parts of my Caminos. In fall of 2013, as usual, she called me to find out if the plans for spring of 2014 were already in preparation. And she immediately specified "no matter where you will be on your birthday, I will definitely come there". Of course, I had already thought about the place where I wanted to celebrate my milestone birthday. My choice had fallen on Toledo. An interesting city that I, unlike Ursula, didn't know yet. Therefore, we planned our Camino stages in a way, that we would arrive in Toledo the day before my 70th birthday and stay three for nights.

Today is the day. I am really looking forward to the arrival of my sister. Ursula already knows her from a Camino last year. Ruth is flying from Zurich to Madrid early morning. From there she will continue by ALSA (a Spanish bus company) to Toledo, and she should be there around noon. Ursula and I walk to the bus station to pick up Ruth. During our greeting and hugging, I suddenly realize that there are two of my best friends standing with us. Walti Häni and his wife Ruth have also traveled here as a 'surprise package', so to speak. They flew together with my sister Ruth and the three of them organized everything without telling me. I can hardly believe it and am overwhelmed.

Toledo is celebrating the 400th anniversary of the death of El Greco (1541-1614) and the exhibition 'El Greco 2014' is currently being held to mark this anniversary. Most hotels are now fully booked. Therefore, my question about accommodation comes posthaste "in which hotel are you staying"? The answer from Walti follows just as quickly, he smiles and says, "guess what"! Great, they have also been able to book a room at the same hotel.

The three of them took the early plane from Zurich to Madrid, which means, they got up very early and have already been traveling for many hours. We catch a cab and drive together to our hotel, where they can check in and freshen up a bit.

Afterwards it is time to look for a restaurant. It is Spanish lunchtime (2 pm), the city is full of locals and tourists and then our party of five arrives at a restaurant. Without a reservation of course! The Restaurante Palacios (also a tip from Thomas Schröder) is centrally located and it is mainly frequented by locals. Exactly to our taste. The whole place with its numerous winding rooms is full, but after a short time we get a table. We enjoy our lunch and of course being together.

After the siesta we meet again. We want to visit the famous church 'Sinagoga Santa Maria la Blanca'. This synagogue from the 12th/13th century was later converted into a church. Inside, it reminds more of a mosque with its Mudéjar decoration.

Near 'Santa Maria La Blanca' is the church 'Iglesia de Santo Tomé'located. Inside hangs the most famous painting of El Greco 'El Entierro del Conde de Orgaz' (Burial of the Count of Orgaz). This painting is the largest painting by El Greco, measuring 4.80 x 3.60 meters.

Since tickets for the El Greco exhibition were no longer available, a visit to this painting is a must on our tour.

Near these two churches, the Museo Victorio Macho can be found. One of the most beautiful museums of Toledo. Due to time constraints, we only visit the sculpture garden with its beautiful view over the Tagus Valley.

On the way to our sightseeing round, I was fortunate enough to get a reservation for the restaurant 'La Orza' for dinner. A table on the terrasse, dignified atmosphere, mild summer night temperatures, among friends and exquisite food. Everything is just perfect, that we forget to take pictures. But the memories will remain!

23 Toledo, Saturday and second rest day

The weather continues to be beautiful and hot. Today we go on different kind of sightseeing tours. Ursula, Ruth, and I walk down to the Tajo River. On the city map we discovered that a hiking and biking path has been built along the river. We follow this beautiful path to a bridge, cross the river and climb up the circular road to the (viewpoint) 'Mirador del Valle'. To the right is the small Ermita Virgen del Valle f4om 17th century. At the entrance door, an azulejo reads 'Aunque pequeña me veis, soy muy grande como ermita, pues la Reina que me habita tiene Toledo a sus pies' (Although you see me small, as a hermitage I am very big, because the queen who lives in me has Toledo at her feet).

To the left of the Ermita is the bar 'Kiosko Base'. This is the bar on the high bank of the Tajo with the magnificent view over Toledo. Perched high on a granite rock above the Tajo loop, is the city with its imposing buildings such as the Cathedral, Museum, Alcázar and the Santa Cruz complex.

After a coffee stop, we board the bus that takes us back across the river to the 'Plaza de Zocodover'.

Afterwards, the three of us stroll through the alleys of the very busy city to the Palacios Restaurant, where we meet up with Walti and Ruth Häni. They have visited Toledo last year on a round trip and have used the morning for their own sightseeing. Lunch again in the restaurant Palacios. We always have a lot to talk about.

Early evening we walk together over the Alcántara Bridge to the panoramic road to the 'Kiosko' Base to enjoy the unique view of Toledo once again, and to end today's beautiful day with an aperitif and tapas.

As I already mentioned with the city of Valencia, one could also intensify the sightseeing of Toledo. But our stay is limited, and we are glad, that we had enough time for the most beautiful sights.

24 Toledo - Torrijos

It is Sunday and it is pilgrimage day again. The three of us, Ursula, Ruth, and I, are standing in front of the hotel at 9:30 a.m. Our backpacks packed. My sister Ruth will pilgrimage with us from here to Zamora. Walti and his wife, also experienced Santiago pilgrims, would love to join us. However, they must travel back to Switzerland today.

Then the cab arrives, which is supposed to take us to a point outside the city. We explain to the driver where we want to go. This is not very easy, because there is neither a village nor a known building there. Simply a concrete bridge in no man's land, which leads over a branch of the Río Guadarrama. There should be a yellow Santiago arrow, that indicates the way out of town. It is always amazing that we, and the cab drivers, find such places at first attempt. Bridge there, yellow arrow there, so, here we go again.

At the beginning it is once again difficult. A large traffic circle, no location information, and no arrows. Help approaches in form of a group of cyclists. I can't just cut them off and so I call out loudly 'por favor, por donde va el Camino de Santiago'? The one at the back of the group stops, greets 'Hola Guapa' (Hello pretty one) and directs us to the national road N-403, later the path is supposed to leave the road at the top right. Muchas Gracias!

According to the book it should be 7 km to Rielves, but it drags on. The way leads through grain fields, which are ready for harvest, but in contrast to the green fields three weeks ago, the grain is now pale-yellow resp. wheat blond. It is over 30° hot and Ruth feels the heat burning down on us relentlessly. In a village along the way a bar is open, a rarity on Sundays at noon. We see that we can fill up our water bottles. Then we set off again to cover the remaining distance.

At 14:30 we reach Torrijos and tend to go immediately for lunch. Watching out for a place to eat, we are directed to Restaurant Tinin and indeed, they offer a good daily menu for 15€.

After having eaten, we walk to the Policia Local station and get the key to the pilgrim hostel, which is in a house across the street. Possibly this was a former parish house. From the large reception room on the first floor, a staircase leads to the second floor. The walls are lined with beautiful azulejos (Spanish wall tiles, mostly in shades of blue). Upstairs are 4 small rooms, each with a bunk bed. Since none of us wants to sleep in the upper bed, we each move into a separate room. We are lucky, no other pilgrims come.

Torrijos - Ávila, 5-day stages, highest point Puerto de El Boqueron, 1315 MüM

The next 5 stages will take us into mountainous areas. We cross on this Camino two of the famous mountain ranges at their foothills. From the southwest, from Plasencia, the Sierra de Gredos extends to San Martin de Valdeiglesias. One stage later, in Cebreros, begins the Sierra de Guadarrama, that continues from there towards the northeast. This area, with its Mediterranean mountain climate, is often used by people of Madrid as a summer resort or for weekends. Consequently, one sees again and again settlements with vacation houses.

The paths follow the course of the terrain and so we come again and again on new hill or mountain ridges. The views ahead give us an idea of what is to come in the next few days. Partly we can see the course of the path in distance, which lets us marvel again and again. But also looks back are worthwhile. Sometimes we stand there and hardly believe how far we have already gone.

25 Torrijos - Escalona

Ursula and I have already been on the road for three weeks and we feel very fit. For my sister, this is only the second day, and therefore we shall abbreviate the stages. While Ursula walks the whole stage, Ruth and drive the first 12 km to Maqueda, and then walk the remaining 12.5 km to Escalona.

Immediately out of Maqueda, the Camino returns to be a natural path in solitude. It is slightly hilly, with beautiful views of the mountains that we will cross in the coming days towards Ávila. Harvested grain fields, large olive plantations, old holm oak forests and dehesas (Dehesa is the Spanish name for grazed oak groves that occupy extensive areas, especially in southwestern Spain) line our path.

We can already feel the announced cold weather front, but it is pleasant to walk. Around noon we can already see the imposing castle of Escalona and soon we reach the small village. First a drink on the pretty Plaza de Infante before we set off on the registration marathon. Policia Local, City Hall and then to our accommodation. It is a casita (small cottage) with 8 beds on a closed school area. It hasn't been cleaned in a long time, so the first thing I do is, to take the broom and begin to mop. First, this is my thanks for the free accommodation and second, I like it clean.
We go back to the village to look for a restaurant. At 2pm Ursula arrives, and we go for lunch. After siesta there is a knock on our door. An elder pilgrim arrives, and he does not seem to be pleased that he must share the accommodation with three women. Later in the evening, the predicted rain front arrives, and it begins to rain.

26 Escalona - San Martin de Valdeiglesias

The route should be divided into two stages, but in between there is no place to stay. So, last night we asked for a ride. There are no buses in this area, and we have booked the only cab in town. Ursula drives to Almorox (7 km) and walks the remaining 24 km from there. Ruth and I drive to El Romillo (14 km) and walk the remaining 16 km from there.

For information, Almorox is the last place in Castilla-La Mancha. Before we shall be walking for many weeks in Castilla y León (largest autonomous region), we will walk today and tomorrow though the autonomous region of Madrid.

Finding the way today is not easy at all. In the outdoor guide is a small map section in which the path crosses the National Road N-403 at the settlement of El Romillo. From there it should go easily up, past countless cattle gates and large granite boulders, 300 m down an earthy firebreak, and so on. Our cab driver had already pointed out that El Romillo was closed in off-season. For us this is ok, because only want to start our walk there. However, there is stupidly no yellow arrow and no shell sign to find. So, we follow the path. Soon a car comes towards us, and I ask for directions. The workers point us back to the National Road, but we don't want to walk on the Road. We continue according to the little plan. Soon we meet an elder couple with a dog. I ask again, and they also want to direct us back to the Carretera. As I read them the directions, translated line by line, the woman suddenly says "Yes that's right. Follow this trail and ignore all turnoffs left and right". We thank her and continue walking as directed. After the firebreak there is another cattle gate and then we reach a small road. In fact, that's where we find the first arrow.

The path is beautiful. It is a nature trail that leads through pine forests with old, gnarled trees and past many imposing granite rocks. Where the forest thins out a bit, we are repeatedly treated to beautiful views into the distance. Around are mountains and valleys. Only three days have passed since we left Toledo and it is amazing how much the environment has changed. From flat meseta with expansive grain fields to wooded hill country. At our first break, I notice that one of my sandals hanging on the outside of my backpack is missing. Following the first impulse, I go back a little, but quickly realize that the place where I took off my jacket is too far back. And now? There are two possibilities:

1. The shoe is on the path and Ursula will find it.
2. the sandal lies in the trunk of the cab.

No matter, currently, I can't do anything. The trail continues up and down the hill, past pine forests, rock roses and lavender. It smells intensely of Mediterranean climate. At 1 p.m. we reach San Martin de Valdeiglesias. We see a billboard of Casa Rural of Adel. We get an apartment for us three and find out it is a good choice. The private house is comfortably furnished, and everything is very clean. At the back of the house there is a gorgeous garden, full of blooming flowers. As Ursula shall arrive much later, Ruth and I go to have lunch and the have our obligatory siesta. Later in the afternoon we meet Ursula, and the trio is complete again.

A little later I track down the cab driver and to my delight he found my sandal in the trunk. Before calling the cab driver, I had to find the Spanish word for trunk in the translation app

Leo. Maletero' - traveling without a car, this word is not necessarily part of your daily vocabulary.

I attach my sandals with carabiner hooks on the outside of the backpack. Until now I knew two types of carabiners. Robust metal ones, which are reinforced with a screw lock. Then the pretty colored ones, lighter, but without a locking mechanism. Typically for me, I had bought the colored carabiners, the ones that matched the turquoise sandals. Somehow this choice shows that even in elder age I can't resist to fashion trends.

In future, I must carefully check every time after a break, whether both sandals are still attached to the backpack.

27 San Martin de Valdeiglesias - Cebreros

During the night it begins to rain heavily. The announced front with precipitation and lower temperatures is here. I had set the alarm clock for 6 o'clock, but because of the rain we get up only at 7 o'clock.

When I am on a pilgrimage and I hear the rain splashing outside early in the morning, I would very much like to just turn over and sleep on. But it helps nothing, a pilgrim wants to go on. Get up, have breakfast, put on rain gear (the first time on this Camino) and at 9 a.m. we start walking. It is only 19 km, i.e., 5 hours.

Today's stage leads first to the Toros of Guisando. These are four large granite sculptures from the 3rd or 4th century, which represent bulls. There is a little detour, but we really want to see this monument. Since markings are missing, we have to ask again and again. We have the feeling to go back and in fact the detour goes back first. After studying the map again, we understand the route. After about an hour we are there and as ordered, the sun shows up. As soon as we have finished photographing, the next rain shower sweeps over us. Then the path follows the country road for a short distance and then turns right. What awaits us now is pure beauty again. Wilderness, lots of noisy birds, beautiful scenery, green pastures, and large granite boulders through which we have to squeeze through in parts. We cross two beautiful Roman bridges from the 12th and 13th century, which are very well preserved because of their remoteness.

Today's destination is Cebreros, located at 750 meters above sea level. At the end of the stage, we follow a steep climb of about 1 hour, which leads us directly to the village center.

After lunch, we set off in search of accommodation. There is no Policia Local here and in the town hall and in the few bars they don't know anything about shelter for pilgrims. Only the Guardia Civil tells us that there is a hotel school in the upper part of the village, and they would take care of the accommodation of the pilgrims. We climb further up and then the surprise. El Rondón is a hotel school on 4-star level. We register, get the key to the Albergue Turistico. Well located, many rooms with up to 6 beds each, modern, good beds, clean sanitary facilities M / F separated. We are positively surprised.

After an unfriendly, even rather dismissive reception in the village, something like that. You never stop learning.
We go down to the village for shopping because tomorrow's stage leads over a high pass and, as in the last days, there is no possibility to stop on the way.

28 Cebreros- San Bartolomé de Pinares

We decided last night to have breakfast at El Rondón. The restaurant opens only at 08:30 and so we can sleep in.

In the morning it is cloudy and cool, but it does not rain. Not for the time being. Today is a mountain stage. According to Outdoor Pilgrim Guide it should be 15 km long, Theo (a pilgrim from Holland, whom I know since 2011 from the Via de la Plata) has noted in his information that it is 18 km, and he walks with GPS.

From the village the path immediately climbs up to the top of the mountain. We follow the small natural paths near a road with little traffic. The vegetation up here consists of crested lavender, broom, and conifers. At the top of the pass with the difficult to pronounce name 'Puerto de Arrebatacapas', the first rain front sweeps over us. Again, and again more rain showers follow. In between, the sun appears briefly, and we use this time to eat our picnic. Further we climb steadily over alpine meadows. I don't know how to describe this area, maybe high pastures? We are on a high plateau with nature trails and a pass road with hardly any traffic. At the top we meet a shepherd with a herd of 300 goats. I like goats, they are refreshingly curious. In addition, goat grazing is an optimal prevention against bushy steep slopes and other sites threatened by bush encroachment.

We have expected to be in about 4 hours at the destination but have disregarded the altitude difference and we need 5 hours. Shortly before the mountain village of San Bartolomé de Pinares, no one would suspect that there was a village here. Only mountains and deep valleys around us. On the opposite side of the valley, there is a village, but the distance is too far for that. Due to some trekking in the Himalayas, I can estimate distance in mountains relatively well.

Huge granite blocks lie scattered around. One large prominent block looks like a 'Popo' from behind. Ursula learns here another Swiss German expression (Füdli) and amuses herself deliciously.

Suddenly the path drops steeply and on a sudden, the path becomes a concrete ramp. Here we are! San Bartolomé de Pinares, 1'039 meters above sea level, a mountain village of 500 souls. As a welcome, a pack of dog's yaps at us. The place looks deserted, but at least it has a bar where we can get something to eat. The pilgrim hostel (Albergue Municipal) is in the building 'Consultorio Medico' (Medical Consultation Center). It has a cramped room with three double bunk beds and there are already three pilgrims here. The men help us put the top three mattresses in the waiting room, and now there is enough room for the three of us. The heating is off, and I think to myself that it will get cold during the night. In the evening it brightens up a bit and we do our obligatory walk around the village. Afterwards we warm up at the bar La Plaza with a warm tea and discuss the plans for tomorrow.

29 San Bartolomé de Pinares - Ávila

Since my first Camino in 2008, I have decided on a daily distance of about 20 to 25 km. I know, for many pilgrims that seems little. They walk 30- 40 km per day and then arrive at the stage place completely exhausted. From a Sherpa in Nepal, my sister and I learned in the 90's that for most physically fit people, a walking time of 5-6 hours is optimal. That means, you rarely come to your limits and still have enough reserves to explore the stage place.

Today's stage would make greater demands on us. According to the outdoor guide, it should be about 28 km long. First, we would have to descend to the village of El Herradón at 918 meters above sea level and then climb 400 meters to the pass 'Puerto de El Boqueron', the highest point on the Camino de Levante.

There is no possibility to split the stage. We inquired last night about a ride up the pass, but the result was negative. There is a bus that leaves for Ávila at 8 a.m. in the morning, but it takes a different route.

The night was very cold and contrary to our hopes, it is again overcast with low clouds over the mountains. Together we decide to skip the stage and go by bus to Ávila. Since we will arrive in Ávila already in the morning, we have enough time to visit this city extensively.

Ávila is the highest city in Spain, located at 1,128 meters above sea level. Worth seeing is the well-preserved city wall, which completely encloses the old city center.

The pilgrim hostel is located near the Roman bridge that crosses the river Adaja. Very centrally located and invitingly furnished. We get a bedroom with 4 beds to ourselves, settle in comfortably, and after the primitive sanitary facilities of last night, we first enjoy a warm shower. In meantime, the clouds have cleared up and the sun begins to shine warmly. After lunch and siesta, we explore the city. We climb the imposing wall, cross the Roman bridge to the 'Mirador Los Quatro Postes', which offers the most beautiful views of the city of Ávila, with the wall and the defense towers. The viewpoint itself, with the 4-meter-high columns, is a special photo motif, especially in the evening light.

Towards evening, it's time to make plans for the two following days, Saturday, and Sunday. We will again be mainly in deserted areas and must buy water and something to eat.

30 Ávila - Gottarendura

We have breakfast in a bar on the opposite side of the Roman Bridge. At 8 o'clock we start walking. The arrows are numerous and very well placed. First, we walk along a country road with hardly any traffic before we can turn off. Then the path leads through a lonely rough area. Granite boulders, holm oaks, crested lavender and cornflowers line our path. In some distance we see a larger lake reservoir.

Half of the route we cross a small settlement and have a coffee at the bar Just before we got there, we saw a bird on a fence that captivated us with its song. I was able to take a picture of it and at the bar I showed the picture to the owner. I knew the Spanish word for nightingale and asked about it. The host didn't know the bird, but another guest asked to see the picture, and yes, it is a ruizseñor (nightingale).

Since Ávila we are walking through the Castilian Plateau. The sky is blue with low-lying cumulus clouds. As soon as we cross over a hill, we are amazed by this endless expanse. Due to the slightly downhill topography, today's 24 km are easily manageable. In 6 hours, we reach the little place Gottarendura, coffee break included. Our kilometer calculation is based on a 4km/hour average. This makes it easier for us to interpret the information in the guide correctly. If it says that the next junction is one kilometer away, we know that we need 15 minutes walking time.

Compared to the information in the Outdoor Guide of 2010, the accommodation situation has changed. The accommodation is now a tourist hostel (no longer a pure pilgrim hostel). We occupy a 3-bed room with private shower. We have lunch in the restaurant of the village. On the menu are 'Alubias blancas' (white beans) and beef stew. Both are delicious.

The French (Philip and Ghislaine) we had met in Tembleque, three stages before Toledo, are also staying here.

Gottarendura is a small village with only 100 inhabitants. The village tour takes less than 10 minutes and so we sit together in the bar in the evening and watch football.

In rural areas of Spain, there is often a small store integrated into the bar, where you can stock up on the essentials. Tomorrow is Sunday and the host explains that he would open the bar only at 11 o'clock. That means, that we have to buy everything necessary for tomorrow this evening, including cups for a quick coffee and yogurt with honey for breakfast.

31 Gottarendura - Arévalo, over 30 km!

We start at 07:50, steel blue sky and fresh 6-8°. The French start with us. Soon we are out in the open again. 2 small villages follow, in which no soul and no dog is on the way. But then we meet an open bar at a gas station. There is a vending machine for coffee and some cookies, not exactly a highlight, but better than nothing.

The path soon crosses a small pine grove where resin is extracted. I inspect the plastic cups on the trunks. I have rarely seen anything like that. After 12 km there is a village on the way with an open bar. We order 'Huevos Fritos con Beicon' (fried eggs with bacon), a real Sunday highlight!

The path leads again through a pine forest with resin containers on the trunks, but this time the forest is large and long. At first, I find it beautiful, but as the distance increases, it becomes boring and colorless. It's like walking through areas with monocultures.

At km 20 we reach the Carretera (country road) and must now follow it to Arévalo. Another 10 km (2 ½ hrs) on sandy paths next to the road and really tiring to walk. It is after 3 p.m. until we reach the outskirts of Arévalo. Since 11:30 we have walked without stopping or sitting down. Whew!!

Normally, things never get hectic for us during the pilgrimage. We have the routes and the distances under control. But today, it is a long stage and on top of that it is Sunday. On Sundays and holidays there is always a certain risk to find open restaurants and stores. We walk faster than usual because we still hope for an open restaurant. Then suddenly, set back from the road a bit, I see a sign 'Asador El Figón' (Asador is a food restaurant). Let's go.

What follows now reads like a parody in retrospect
A large eatery, loud buzz of voices and still all the tables full. Waiters skillfully moving between the tables and serving food and drink. Families chatting animatedly and children walking around exuberantly.
And then the three of us stand there. Dusty, sweaty, with backpacks, in hiking boots, and our faces still slightly red from the exertion - a strong contrast to all the elegantly dressed Spanish guests.

One of the waiters approaches us and asks for our wishes. We ask whether we could probably still get something to eat. His answer - yes, sure, wait a minute, I'll get a table ready for you. All the tension of the last half hour is gone, we stand there quietly and think, what luck!

After a short wait, a hand signal from the back of the room and we are asked to a freshly set table. We are first asked for our drink preferences, and then given a menu to delve into the food on offer. First the drinks are brought (in Spain there is always a big bottle of water) and then we order our food. This is followed by the refreshment break. I must wash my hands and rinse off my face. I don't like the salty skin on my face.

When all three of us are sitting at the table, the spirits come back. We talk about the route, what each of us has seen and possibly photographed, about our thoughts while walking, etc.

And when starters and main course are served, there is a 'voracious silence' (we learned this from Bernd on the Camino Francés in 2009). The food tastes great and we are satisfied.

Around 5 pm we walk to our booked hostal in the center of town and are glad to have arrived. The siesta must be cancelled today, because after showering and washing, we must start making plans for the following day.

Unfortunately, after such long stages, we lack time and energy to visit the town.

32 Arévalo - Medina del Campo

The stage from Arévalo to Medina del Campo would be again 32 km. The Camino runs the entire length near the A-6 highway and the Madrid-Galicia railroad line. Not right next to it, but still close.

Half a year ago, at the beginning of our planning, Ursula told me on the phone, that near Medina del Campo is the 'Castillo de Fonseca, also called Castillo de Coca'. From one of her many books with the most beautiful castles and palaces of Spain, she had known the castle of Coca for decades, but had never had the opportunity to visit it. We both agreed that we would take the possibility to visit it. On one hand, we always consider our age, because we don't know how much longer we will be able to make such unusual trips, and on the other hand, every now and then an alternative pilgrimage day is allowed. Today is one of those!

Arévalo - Coca - Medina del Campo is like a triangle on the map. We go by cab 30 km in direction of Segovia. The drive across the Castilian plateau is worth seeing. Castillo de Coca is an imposing brick castle in Mudejar style, built in the 15th century and it can be visited. In Spain, museums are usually closed on Monday, but thanks to the Internet I knew that Castillo de Coca is open on Monday.

Two towers are open, and we can admire the interesting restorations of the Mudejar style azulejos. The castle is also impressive from the outside and in good weather there are impressive pictures.

While we visit the castle, our driver is waiting for us. For him it is a nice drive overland, which he can't drive every day like this.

For us, this trip was absolutely worth it. We have visited a magnificent building and our bodies could recover from yesterday's exertion on the ride through this unique landscape.

After the sightseeing, the journey continues 30 km to the northwest. In Medina del Campo we spot a hostal and ask for a room. The owner would have one free but has a telephone reservation for the room. He does not dare to give us the room and so we go to the monastery and spend the night with the padres. Three single cells with one bed each, good and clean. Such overnight stays always make the uniqueness of a pilgrimage. Who can say of himself that he has spent the night in a monastery?

In Medina del Campo is thr monument to Queen Isabella La Católica. She spent many years of her life in this city and died in Medina del Campo in 1504. Isabella I of Castile, also called Isabella the Catholic, was Queen of Castile and León from 1474 to 1504 as well as Queen of Aragon from 1479 to 1504 as the wife of Ferdinand II.

33 Medina del Campo - Nava del Rey

Today we walk through a very different area and topography, it is slightly hilly and the path winds through little used area. We walk along an old railroad line, and I think to myself that no trains run here anymore. But a wrong thought, then suddenly, a lonely small train composition chugs on its way.

We pass a remote sheep farm and a pasture with cows. In a hamlet we take a rest at the village weighbridge. Then the path crosses the construction site of the future AVE line Madrid - Galicia, 'Alta Velocidad Española' (Spanish High-Speed Train). The railroad line Madrid - Zamora should be ready in 2015. Zamora - Orense, however, only in 2022.

At some point, two men approach us on their jogging lap. This is rarely seen as we meet mostly women on their Nordic walking or jogging training rounds. Soon we can see the church tower of Nava del Rey from a slight hill. After 12 o'clock we are already there. According to the pilgrimage guide, we could spend the night in the Capuchin convent, but they no longer accept pilgrims. So, we get rooms in the centrally located Hostal Zamora.

In Nava del Rey is the large church Los Santos Juanes from the 16th century with a sacristy worth seeing. The director of the tourist office shows us the church in a private tour. From him we also learn that large parts of the village are undercut with wine cellars. In former times a lot of wine was grown here, and some cellars are still used today.

34 Nava del Rey - Castronuño

During the night it rained heavily once again. I saw some drops in my weather APP but did not believe in rain. The alarm clock was set for 06.15, but in view of the wet weather we decide to have breakfast only at 8 o'clock. Finally, we start walking in rain gear. The light is in shades of gray, but the path is still beautiful and easy to walk. At the beginning rather flat, then it slowly becomes hilly. After 2 hours we come through a village and would like to have a coffee, but the bar does not open until 1pm. At the tienda (store) we buy bread and cheese and eat half of these crispy rolls on a bench next to the church. It is cool and so the break is rather short.

Now follows an extremely varied route. Soon we are in a side valley of the river Duero. It has lots of poppies and cornflower fields and the land is very green. At 13.30 we arrive are in Castronuño, our today's stage place. During the telephone registration yesterday the Hospitalera asked me to call her when we are there. Because it is raining, she picks us up in her car at the beginning of the village, and on the way to the pilgrim hostel she takes us on a tour of the village. Castronuño is located on a prominent bend of the Duero River. The pilgrim hostel is new, has 9 bunk beds and for the time being opens only as needed. The two Spaniards and the Finn have already arrived at the hostel (the three from San Bartolomé de Pinares). It is always special not to see pilgrims for days and then suddenly meet them again at a stage place. One exchanges with each other and learns that they have made a detour or spent a day of rest in a place.

Towards evening the rain stops. We go for a walk around the village and visit the church from the 13th century, which stands on the hill above the Duero loop. We let our eyes wander over the lazily moving river. Dark storm clouds hang over the river valley, somehow mystical. When I stand on the banks of the Río Duero, it's like coming home for me.

Assignment as Hospitalera Voluntaria in pilgrim hostels
On my first Caminos, I admired the great commitment of the Hospitalero/as in charge. They welcome the arriving pilgrims with much empathy, although they have long presence hours. What you don't see is the incredibly strict working hours in the morning as soon as the pilgrims have left the house. Here it is necessary to clean the whole house within a very short time and bring it in shape. Then showering, washing, shopping, eating and being ready again at 1 or 2 p.m. to receive the newly arriving pilgrims. As a Hospitalero/a, one is primarily responsible for organizational matters, but it is equally important to have an open ear for the concerns of the pilgrims. And be it just to listen.

During my 2nd Camino, I had planned to volunteer at a Spanish pilgrim hostel the following year as a thank you for the many nights spent in 'Albergue de Peregrinos' (pilgrim hostels).

In late fall of 2009, I took the necessary steps and in spring of 2010 I completed the training course in Logroño. After the course, I did my first assignment as Hospitalera Voluntaria in Ponferrada. After that I was once in Grañon and twice in Zamora. In Zamora I felt very comfortable from the beginning and that is why it is like coming home for me.

The missions last half a month each. In Ponferrada there are about 5 Hospitalero/as since this hostel has 180 beds. Zamora has only 32 beds, but most of the time you are alone. Grañon, a cult hostel on the Camino Francés has about 60 beds and the two Hospitalero/as also cook for and with the pilgrims in the evenings. Also, a wonderful experience.

Since I decided to walk the long Camino de Levante in spring 2014, I knew that I would not have time to do another assignment in a pilgrim hostel.

35 Castronuño - Toro

The night was rather restless. Not because of snoring noises, but because one of the men apparently had restless legs, and it constantly rustled strongly due to the plastic mattress covers.

Up at 06:30. Yesterday late in the evening it rained heavily again, but this morning it is dry. The Hospitalera told us yesterday that the path today will be over hills, up and down. For the first time we see a huge 'water dragonfly' in action. In meantime, I know what these things are called. They are irrigation trucks, which irrigate the large fields cultivated with grain or vegetables with water. Impressive! When the path passes very close to these irrigation trucks, we must time it exactly not to be surprised by a downpour.

After about 1 ½ hours we reach the village of Villafranca del Duero and allow ourselves a late breakfast. We order again our beloved Pan tostado con tomate and get for the first time simply 2 slices of toast, each with a slice of tomato. Breakfast-wise, we have definitely arrived in central Spain. Here, only toast with butter and jam is served as breakfast.

Up and down the hills we continue, passing fertile fields. At some point we sit down at a water station to eat our bocadillo. In the water basin we see a snake. Later, we learn from the French couple that Philip went down into the basin and saved the snake.

Today we will reach Toro. I am very excited about this city. Before Toro, an imposing pre-Romanesque bridge (Puente Mayor) is crossed and then the steep climb begins. As soon as we arrive at the Plaza Mayor, the sun shows up. A great welcome.

Toro has no pilgrim hostel, but you can stay overnight in the monastery. But we are too early for that and decide for a hostal at the main square. Lunch, shower, wash, siesta. The usual pilgrim routine.

After the siesta, another highlight of this Camino awaits us. The visit of the famous church 'La Colegiata Santa María la Mayor' from the 12th century in Romanesque-Gothic style. Absolutely worth seeing is the 'Portada de la Majestad' (west portal), a masterpiece of the Gothic period in Castile. Marvel and take pictures. However, Toro is not only known for its famous church and its imposing location high above the Río Duero. In recent years, Toro has become the trendy region in terms of excellent wines. Toro red wines are dark, almost black, and taste full-bodied.

In early evening the French arrive here, tired from an overlong stage. We meet later for a glass of Toro red wine with tapas and talk animatedly in 2 languages (French and English).

Tomorrow they will walk through 37 km to Zamora, while we have planned another overnight stay in Villalazán.

36 Toro - Villalazán

The second last stage before Zamora. Descending from Toro to the banks of the Río Duero, the trail first passes the red wall. Impressive. The route is varied. We cross the Toro-Zamora canal, the Medina del Campo - Zamora railroad line and then also the iron bridge over the Río Duero. Afterwards we find ourselves in intensively cultivated agricultural areas, where potatoes, corn, grain and lettuce are planted. With us on the way is also the French couple. Together we sit down for a picnic and then say goodbye to them. Since they have not planned any rest days in Zamora, we will probably not see them again.

The road then runs for a long 6 km on a country road. We are glad to be in Villalazán around noon. The accommodation is located in a girls' school, and we are allowed to stay in the kindergarten room. I use the free afternoon to complete my travel notes and there is also time to draft the text for my next Camino mail to my friends.

37 Villalazán - Zamora

Once again, we must leave without breakfast. It is Saturday and the only bar in town opens only around noon. Exit village, on the road, two thick arrows point to the left on a natural path. We follow them, although the description in the guide says we should follow the carretera (country road).

The arrows were wrong and so we walked 2 km too much. Back on the Carretera. After a while the path leads through a jungle-like piece along the Río Duero. The path is almost overgrown, but from time to time a lonely arrow shows that we are still on the right way. At the end of this forest, a steep climb follows, and the signposts (arrows) are completely missing. We walk along the trail to the next visible village for a coffee. No fresh bread nor crackers, fortunately we still have our 'Lomo Bocadillo' from yesterday.

Then follows a beautiful part along the Toro-Zamora-Canal. Broom, poppies, daisies, and cornfields surround us. At noon we reach Zamora. Since the last part of the way was along the Río Duero, we can take a selfie of our arrival on the 'Puente Romano' (Romanesque stone bridge with 16 arches).

It's feels good to be back here. A short climb to the Plaza Mayor and then a Copita de Verdejo as a welcome aperitif.

Since we will be here for 2 nights, we stay in a hostal, which I already know for years. A very warm welcome. Then follow food, siesta, and stroll through the city. As a luxury we feel the offer of the hostal operators to wash our laundry in the machine. We accept with thanks. In the evening we have a Manzanilla (chamomile tea) on the Plaza Mayor.

Now we have the feeling that we have really arrived.
With Zamora, Ursula and I have reached a large section of our Camino. Ruth has reached her destination here and shall fly back the day after tomorrow.

Lomo Bocadillo (cutlet bread)
A few years ago, I was on the Via de la Plata with my sister. At a stage place a large village celebration was held. In the only, totally overcrowded restaurant, we nevertheless got an early dinner. Starter: a big plate of pasta with tomato sauce (pasta is a rarity for Spain). Main course: Per person 4 Schnitzel Lomo (for us these are pork schnitzel from the kidney piece) with potatoes. Since on the long stage on the following day no place and consequently also no stop would be possible, we decided shortly decided to make sandwiches with 2 remaining Schnitzels per person and to pack. From that day on, our Lomo Bocadillo was invented. During all our Caminos we always get way too big portions and instead of supporting food waste, we eat it the following day on the road. It always tastes very good.

38 Rest Day in Zamora

A beautiful morning awaits us. Breakfast at Café Teatro. The theater across the street is finally finished restored after being a big construction site from 2011 to 2013.

Zamora is a small town with about 60'000 inhabitants, located at an altitude of 660 meters above sea level. Due to its numerous Romanesque churches, it is also called the Romanesque Museum. The Romanesque 'Catedral de San Salvador' (Cathedral) dates to the 12th century and looks unique with its dome roof made of imitation shingles. It stands in middle of the old town of Zamora, on a hill above the Río Duero.

In Zamora two great Caminos de Santiago meet. One is the Via de la Plata, which leads from Seville to Astorga via Salamanca and Zamora, or from Granja de Moreruela westward via Puebla de Sanabria to Santiago. The lesser known is the Camino de Levante, the one we walked. It leads from Valencia via Toledo, Ávila and Toro to Zamora, and from there over the Camino Sanabrés via Ourense to Santiago de Compostela.

We use our rest day to do a few things. To the bus station to buy the bus ticket for Ruth's trip tomorrow to Madrid airport. Ursula and I will continue our Camino tomorrow towards north and we might need some provisions. Around noon we go to a restaurant at the Plaza del Maestro to have lunch on the terrace. Here we also meet Vicente, a pilgrim from Malaga, whom we have met again and again since Toledo.

After our siesta, we walk to the pilgrim hostel to get the stamp for our second Credencial (pilgrim's passport).

We then visit the cathedral and then continue down to the river (Río) Duero to photograph the ancient oil mills. A final stroll up to the small square closed to the church of San Cipriano follows, with a superb view over Puente Romano and the countless stork nests all around.
To finish this relaxing stay, we sit down for a nightcap on the terrace of the Parador, where we round off this beautiful day, and enjoy the pastel-colored evening atmosphere over the Río Duero.

Paradores is a Spanish state-owned hotel chain. Most Paradores are located in historically significant places and/or buildings. Mostly in gorgeous landscapes and often offer a spectacular view.

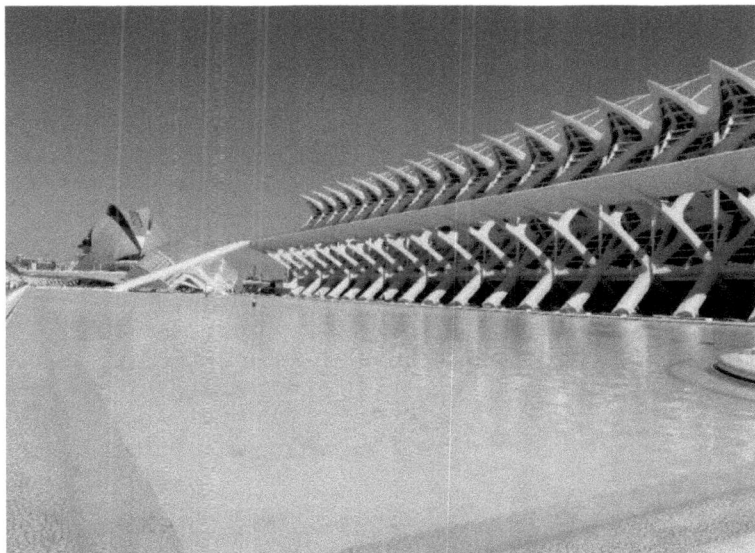

↑Valencia, Ciudad Artes y Ciencias / Orange trees↓

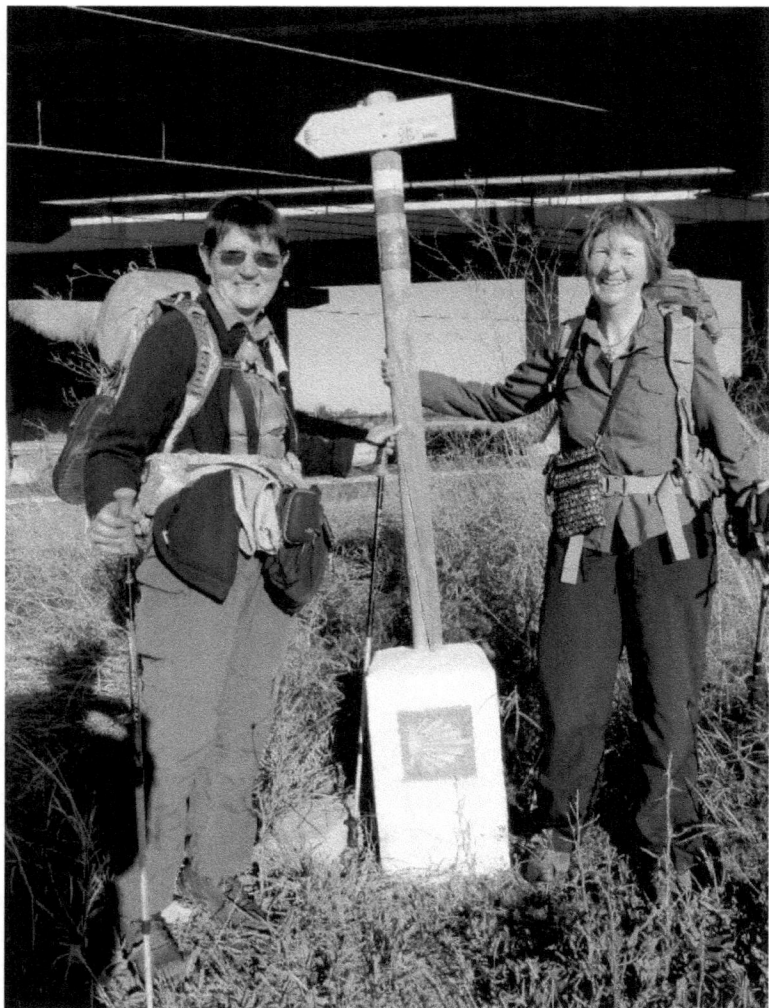

↑ Ursula Austermann and Margrit Wipf ↑

First day of our pilgrimage across Spain

↑Poppy road in cornfield / flowers on the way↓

↑ Persian lilac / garlic fields ↓

↑ Toledo / On the way in the Sierra de Gredos ↓

↑ Ávila with the imposing city wall / Castillo de Coca ↓

↑ Trails can also be demanding / in rain gear ↓

↑ Toro, view of the Roman bridge / Red rocks ↓

Arrival in Zamora

PART TWO

ZAMORA - SANTIAGO

DE COMPOSTELA

Spanish language with 'dialects and facets
In this book I use Spanish expressions again and again. Since my youth I have been interested in foreign countries and languages. After my first two foreign languages during school (French and Italian) and a one-year language stay in Ticino, I started learning Spanish at the age of 18. First private lessons. Later, on my many trips to countries where Spanish is spoken, I steadily expanded my knowledge of the language.

In restaurants and bars in Spain nowadays there are large screens that constantly show the latest news. In addition, newspapers with national and local information are available and so my vocabulary is constantly expanding.
Ursula also speaks this language fluently. She also has an extensive vocabulary and excellent knowledge of Spanish history, culture, and literature.

This makes it easy for the two of us to get in touch with locals and we always learn new and interesting things. On a pilgrimage path like the Camino Francés, you can easily converse in English. On Caminos like the Camino de Levante, you should have a reasonably good knowledge of the language. Otherwise, you might miss so much.

Ever since I have been in Spain for 2 months in spring, at the end of my stay in this country, I always go to the big bookstore on Rúa do Vilar in Santiago de Compostela and buy a book in Spanish. Either I already know exactly which book I want to buy, or I get inspired. For Barcelona lovers I find 'La Catedral del Mar' by Ildefonso Falcones very worth reading. Of course, I don't always understand every word, but, when I read a book in a foreign language, I understand the meaning of the text. Only when the word appears a few times in a row do I look it up in the dictionary or translation App.

The official language in Spain is Castellano (Spanish or Castilian). In addition, there are three other languages: Gallego (Galician), Catalan (Catalan) and Vasco (Basque), which are the languages of the autonomous communities of Galicia, Catalonia, and the Basque Country.

Until the beginning of the 1980s, 'Castellano' (Spanish) clearly dominated in public sphere. Buildings, streets, signs, etc. were written exclusively in Spanish. Castellano is still understood and spoken throughout Spain, but today there is practically a state of bilingualism in the Autonomous Communities mentioned above. In Santiago de Compostela, for example, it is no longer written 'Plaza de Galicia' but 'Praza de Galicia'.

39 Zamora - Montamarta

Ruth left this morning and is on her way back to Zurich. Ursula and I set off again on the Camino.

The two stages from Zamora to Montamarta and Granja de Moreruela lead through a pot-flat landscape, dead straight north. The area is called 'Tierra del Pan' (Land of Bread). As the translation suggests, the main crop grown in this area is grain. The grain fields have different shades of color, from pale yellow to beige, depending on the type of grain and on the stage of growth.

Up to the village Roales del Pan, the way is not spectacular. To cheer up we see at the beginning of Roales in a garden large fantasy figure of pilgrims. On all sides one sees the wide horizon, there are no mountains and hills and on the earthy slope one could believe oneself on the moon. Unfortunately, there is nowhere to sit down for a break, so we have to stand on feet on our drink stop. Shortly before Montamarta, our today's stage goal, we cross the AVE route, which contains however still no rails. AVE is the Spanish high-speed train, and in this area, its being built for the route from Madrid to Galicia.

Far ahead of us goes a single pilgrim, otherwise we see no one for over 4 hrs. The Camino is very well marked.

Around noon we are already in Montamarta, a small village. The pilgrim hostel on the outskirts of Montamarta, where we wanted to spend the night, has been closed since October 2013. From a farmer on his big tractor, we get the information that there are overnight accommodations in the village. We should inquire at the Super Mercado. There we get the tip for a Casa Rural nearby.

Casa Rurales are country houses or vacation homes. These houses are rented by the room or completely. Partly the owners live in the house with private area.

The Casa Rural in Montamarta rents rooms for 40€ per double room. On the upper floor there is also a dormitory with 8 beds, for 15€ per bed. Since we are the first pilgrims, we decide for 2 beds in the dormitory. The house has a large 'patio' (inner courtyard) with chairs and umbrellas. For lunch we walk to the village and afterwards we lie down for a siesta.

Later, quite a few pilgrims arrive here. From today we will be with a larger number of pilgrims, since most pilgrims choose the same stage lengths.
We are the only ones of the Camino de Levante, and we don't know the other pilgrims yet. Later we learn from them that they all walked the Via de la Plata from Sevilla. A Camino that we both have walked in earlier years.

When you often stay in pilgrim hostels, you quickly develop preferences for the location of the bed. Soon you also know about the different habits of the various nationalities. Germans and Swiss like it when the air can circulate in the rooms and therefore keep the windows open. Southerners, as Spanish and Italian pilgrims, usually close all windows and then there is soon a stuffy air in the dormitory. Whenever possible or available, I choose a lower bed against a wall or window. I quickly realized that the one who sleeps by the window has control over the air quality in the dormitory.

Pilgrim encounters and friendships

From my own experience, but also from the stories of other pilgrims I have met over the years, the pattern of getting to know each other is usually the same. At the beginning its just Hello or buen Camino. After a few days, walking the same stages you begin to know each other, and then growing together into a 'pilgrim family'. Pilgrim groups are multinational and often multilingual. Speaking several languages results in many interesting conversations.

40 Montamarta - Granja de Moreruela

I had decided yesterday to go by bus to Riego del Camino and walk only the remaining 7 km. The reason for this: According to the latest information, there is a major construction site on this path for the highway A-66 (Autovia Ruta de la Plata from Seville to the north coast).

It's a pity, because after Montamarta to the west, the big reservoir 'Embalse de Ricobayo' can be seen. On a detailed map of the province of Zamora, one can see that this large and ramified reservoir is fed by the Río Esla. The 285 km long Río Esla rises in the Cantabrian Mountains and flows through the provinces of Léon and Zamora. Finally, it flows into the Río Duero at Muelas del Pan (about 30 km west of Zamora). In three days, we will cross the Río Esla over an impressive bridge.

Ursula has already started at 06:20 and I stand at 07 o'clock at the Carretera and wait for the bus. The bus t drives 10 min later past me. Since I had assumed that the bus would not stop on the busy Carretera, I stood at a bus shelter on the wrong side of the road. Wrong thought. Back to the Casa Rural and ask for another transport possibility. A little later I am in Riego del Camino and start walking from here. The trail from here is beautiful and well signposted. I only have to walk the last part through the large construction site.

Granja de Moreruela is a small town separated by the busy national road N-630. It is possible that later the traffic will shift to the highway, but only if this highway can be used toll-free. Otherwise, the trucks will continue to drive on the national road, and nothing will change for the village.

In Granja there used to be a simple pilgrim's hostel with only 10 beds, and this has always caused space problems, since at this time of the year there are usually about 30 pilgrims walking the same stages. Now there is a new hostel with 20 beds on the other side of the Carretera. Good, clean and with nice sanitary facilities. On the ground floor it has 4 bunk beds and on the 1st floor a room with 6 bunk beds and a lounge.

Since I only walked 7 km today, I sit down in shade of the terrasse and write more detailed information in my travel diary.

When Ursula arrives later, she tells me that she had to walk partly through bad dirt on the large construction site of the Autovia. Yes, such bad passages can be encountered every now and then and so far, we have been really lucky on this Camino.

In pilgrim hostels you prepare your bed after arrival. The mattresses are usually covered with a plastic cover, and you put your sleeping bag on it. This then means that this bed is occupied.

After Ursula has prepared her bed, we go to have lunch.

All pilgrims from yesterday evening are also at the Granja de Moreruela hostel, but unlike us, they eat mainly in the evening.

Preparation for tomorrow's stage. We both know this stage from previous years quite well. I walked it in fall of 2011 with my sister and Ursula knows it from spring of 2009. The trail from Garnja de Moreruela to Tábara is 27 km long and it has, until shortly before arrival, neither water points nor food possibility. We therefore must carry enough water and some food provisions with us.

Food & Drink

At the beginning of the book, I told you that we eat lunch whenever possible, so we mainly opt for the daily menu.

In most restaurants there are also 'Raciónes' (in Switzerland this is called à la Carte). With these offers from the menu, we choose the individual dishes separately. Everything is put separately on the bill, and in addition, in Spain, cover, bread, water and tapas are charged. This quickly sums up to 20€, usually twice as much as the daily menu. However, Raciónes also have an advantage. You can share them (compartir) and try different dishes instead of having to choose just one.

On our rest days we like to be surprised by the diversity and delicacies of the regions. We are usually in Spring on the Caminos, and I often have the feeling that I am walking through the vegetable garden of all of Europe.

It's amazing how many vegetables are planted. The Spaniards eat a lot of meat and unfortunately there are rarely vegetables on the menu. But if once there is Verdura a la Plancha (grilled vegetables) or for example fried artichokes, I don't have to think for long.

Besides meat, there is also fish or seafood on the menu. Ursula often chooses the fish menu and most of the time it is Merluza (hake). I never thought about why Merluza is always offered on the daily menu until I saw a TV program about fishing on Spain's Atlantic coasts. The peak season for catching Merluza is in spring and that's when we're out on the Caminos.

41 Granja de Moreruela - Tábara

After a few nights in Hotels, I must get used to sleeping in a dormitory, together with strangers. The night was consequently so-so-la-la.

We start walking at 06:20. Easy walking on nice wide paths. The landscape has changed tremendously. Green shrubs and holm oaks as far as the eye can see. Gone is the monotonous flat Meseta.

From today on we go straight westward, and the sun is in our back during the whole morning. The temperature is pleasant and the markings on the trails are good. After about 2 hrs. we reach the Río Esla (river Esla) in the valley of the same name.

The Pilgrim's Guide says that the original path branches off to the left just after the bridge. But from far away you can see only a rock wall. Where should there be a path? But, after crossing the imposing granite bridge, the arrows actually point through the rocks to an adventurous path to the riverbank. Wildly romantic! Soon, a steep climb out of the gorge onto a hill follows. This is an ideal resting place to admire the course of the river in more detail and to take pictures. I could sit here for hours and just watch the river go by. This area is also known for the large bird migrations that pass through here in fall on their way south.

After the break, the path zigzags through holm oak forests, past a lonely finca with an imposing entrance, and then slowly descending from the hill to the plain. From afar, you can see the path going dead straight towards Faramontanos de Tábara.

Some distance in front of us other pilgrims are walking. Suddenly we see them running with their heavy backpacks. The reason is a big sprinkler system that irrigates the surrounding fields. Ah, we will have to take a good look at that. Because although it's already hot, we don't feel like taking a shower.

With such installations, my practical disposition comes into play. After all, these sprinklers must follow a clear pattern and move in the set rhythm. But they don't always do that. I then wait until the water jet is over and think that I should just run fast now. Most of the time it works, but there are also sprinklers with variable rhythm, where each time at the critical moment the water jet changes its direction. Today we are lucky, and we get through without getting wet.

In Faramontanos de Tábara a small bar is temporarily open and here we are also lucky. A short stay, a drink and something small to eat. Then we go on. On the next section you can see the enormous terrain shifts due to the work on the AVE railroad line.

In Tábara we are expected. When I did my volunteer work in the pilgrims' hostel of Zamora in spring of 2011, Carlos, a Hospitalero Voluntario from Zamora, supported me every day during the most rigorous hours. Today he is in the area and awaits us at the bar of the Hotel for a drink and tapas. It's nice to be able to meet spontaneously with friends far away.

42 Tábara - Santa Croya de Tera

At breakfast, a Spaniard explained today's route to two pilgrims. We are only half listening.

On the way, an arrow painted over in green color, suddenly points to the left. For us this is the wrong direction. We two are the first in this pilgrim convoy (two Spanish and three Dutch) and are undecided which arrows we should follow. We wait for the two Spaniards and then decide to follow the green arrow. First over the high AVE bridge and then up the hill. Now I suddenly remember the trail from 2011. The path slowly winds its way up a hillside. We are in an original landscape of trees and bushes. I turn around often and look at the distance covered. Beautiful views and nice to walk. The range of hills separates the wide valley of Tábara from the 'Tierra del Tera' (land of the river Tera).

After about 3 hours the trail divides. Both paths are marked with the Camino de Santiago sign. We walk straight ahead because I remember that there was a bar on the way. And it is still like that today. Sitting comfortably in the sun and drinking a coffee, for Ursula and me this is simply part of the pilgrimage. Afterwards, the path is different than in 2011, but much nicer. Someone took great pleasure to guide us pilgrims from the small side road onto a beautiful nature path. Thank you!

In Santa Croya de Tera is the private hostel, 'Casa Anita'. A beautiful facility with a flowery garden and exceptionally friendly welcome. Everything is clean, good food and cozy togetherness with the other pilgrims.

In the neighboring municipality of Santa Marta de Tera is a Romanesque church from the 13th century with the oldest known representation of St. James as a pilgrim (Santiago Peregrino).

Because tomorrow's stage will be very long again, we walk to Santa Marta de Tera in late afternoon to visit the church and the Santiago statue. Although Ursula and I have already looked at the church in previous years, but on a Camino such devotional moments are simply a must.

43 Santa Croya de Tera - Rionegro

A fantastically beautiful stage leads through a wild natural landscape along the Río Tera. Many parts of the route I no longer know. Where trails used to lead through the thicket, there are now well-kept paths with very good designation. Then follows the ascent to the large dam wall and we reach the elongated reservoir Embalse de Nuestra Señora de Agavanzal. The Camino leads along the right bank.

I have vivid memories of this section of the trail. I usually walk the Caminos de Santiago in spring. But in 2011, I walked the 1st half of the Via de la Plata in spring and the 2nd half the same year in September. It was a hot autumn. At this lake, there are several places to swim, and the water was tempting. I would have loved to cool off in the refreshing water at that time, but my sister and an acquaintance were already far ahead. Since both were on the way without cell phone, I unfortunately had to walk also further. If I should ever be on this Camino again in September, I would announce my bathing wishes in advance!

After the passage by the lake, the area resembles a savannah. I like it very much. We also make rapid progress. The weather is nice, and the partly stormy winds give us a pleasant temperature. But I feel slight pain in my left foot!!! These are the effects of the last days with long stages and too fast pace. I must take better care of myself. As we continue, I decide to go by bus for the greater part of the route tomorrow, to spare my foot in early stages of a possible tendinitis.

In meantime, we have become part of a Camino Sanabrés pilgrimage group. After about 30 km, we arrive in Rionegro del Puente around 3 pm. We check in and choose our beds on the upper floor of the spacious hostel and then go to lunch. Afterwards shower, wash, siesta.

Tomorrow's stage would be again 30 km long and so I order, in absence of a bus connection, a transport for the first 20 km. The three Dutchmen also want to join me, because in their stage planning, they lack of one day.

Tendinitis resp. tendon inflammations: Many pilgrims suffer from it. Tendinitis is an acute irritation of the tendon due to overload. Long stages, at fast pace, too little training or no rest days lead again and again to this annoying pain. Treatments of rest, relief and anti-inflammatory measures usually help. However, if you ignore the pain, you may soon be unable to walk at all and must take a break for a week. No pilgrim wants that. So, it's a matter of shifting down a gear early on and possibly swallowing anti-inflammatory medication.

44 Rionegro del Puente - Palacios de Sanabria

During the night it was raining very hard but at 6 o'clock the rain stops. Ursula decides to walk the 30 km to Palacios de Sanabria.

The three Dutchmen and I eat our breakfast in the bar of Rionegro. Afterwards, the owner of the bar drives us to Asturianos, as agreed last night.

Dark clouds hang on the sky over Asturianos, a small town on the way. The three Dutchmen (Cornelius and a couple who are friends) and I put on the rain gear. The path leads through grassland and is now wet and muddy. Nature has changed again. In meantime, there are more fruit trees, apples and pears and now also big chestnut trees. After about an hour we reach the small hamlet of Palacios de Sanabria, the stage stop for Ursula and me. The three Dutchmen continue today to Puebla de Sanabria.

Since it can still take hours until Ursula arrives, I first go to our reserved accommodation. It is a private house in which the owner offers hostel and double rooms. In between the sun is shining and I take the opportunity to wash my long pants and hang them outside. Since it is rather cool, I then retire to our room and read in my travel diary. Soon I fall asleep. Are these the effects of the anti-inflammatory drugs? Later I get up, walk to the bar, and wait for Ursula. Around 3 p.m. she is there, and we enjoy a simple but tasty lunch.

45 Palacios de Sanabria - Puebla de Sanabria

During the night I had seen a beautiful starry sky, but in the morning, it is gray again. We have ordered breakfast at 8 o'clock, because it is only 11 km to Puebla de Sanabria. We start in Fleece and Goretex jacket, but soon can take off one of the jackets. There are beautiful paths through mixed forests and past abandoned villages with stone houses that are deteriorating into ruins. Actually a pity, considering how much work, time, and effort the former owners had invested in the construction of these solid houses. We also pass through the village of Otero de Sanabria. Above the church portal there is a relief of a purgatory worth seeing.

Since we are in the valley of the Río Tera, we walk again in a direct line from east to west. To the south is the large branching reservoir 'Embalse de Cernadilla' and only a few kilometers south is the Spanish / Portuguese border.

Puebla de Sanabria is situated slightly elevated above the valley. It is a small town with a picturesque center. Worth visiting is the beautiful Romanesque church from the 12th century 'Nuestra Señora del Azogue' with the main portal, and there are also the imposing castle towers over the valley. Because of the location and the sights, Puebla de Sanabria has lots of tourists. The accommodation prices are therefore slightly upscale.

Around noon we arrive and start looking for a Hostal in the upper village. The place is as if deserted. Of course, it is Sunday, and the season has not yet begun. The first hostal is closed and the second is under renovation. Looking for a place to stay, we come to a hotel that has attracted attention since Tábara by intrusive billboards. Not necessarily our favorite, but in absence of an alternative we inquire about a room. Everything is fine, comfortable room, good location and the price is also ok. We move into our room and go shopping while the stores are still open.

During the next few days, we will again be mostly in areas without large towns on the road. After shopping, it is already time for lunch. It is not easy to find a restaurant that offers more than just tapas. But we find one. Mesón Abelardo, a typical restaurant, is perfect for us. We get one of the last free tables and enjoy a very good meal. My appetizer is delicious 'Revuelto de Ajetes' (scrambled eggs with young or summer garlic). For my main course, I order 'Albóndigas caseras' (meatballs made with a home recipe). This is one of my favorite dishes in Spain, but only if they are well prepared. Over the years I have become a connoisseur of this dish. At home I have a very good Spanish recipe for albóndigas and cook them every now and then.

After the siesta, we take a tour of the village. The alleys of the village center are characterized by two-story stone houses with picturesque and flower-covered balconies.

46 Puebla de Sanabria - Lubián

The breakfast is good and in addition, each pilgrim is given a packed lunch with bocadillo and some fruit. The stage leads over the Padornelo Pass (1'360 m above sea level). This is the highest point on the Camino de Levante. Due to the construction works on the AVE route, the original, but also exhausting, route has become even more difficult. As an alternative the way is led over the old pass road. Although we are not necessarily friends of road routes, we decide for this variant. The valley of Sanabria narrows increasingly and on both sides, it now has high mountains. We start from Requejo. The path is beautiful and leads through enchanted forests. First flat then slowly rising. At some point we come to the old pass road and now follow this alternative. After the pass we continue on the road.

In fall of 2011, the path branched off the road at some point and followed an old trail. Very nice paths, partly along a water channel, but also stony and rather difficult to walk. Along the way we passed the small hamlet of Aciberos with some stone houses and an old water mill from the 15th century.

Today, in spring 2014, this path is unfortunately no longer passable. Striking orange signs indicate a 'deviation' (rerouting). Moreover, it is forbidden to follow the original path, as blasting works for the AVE are still in progress.

Consequently, we must walk on a new road section, which is bordered on both sides by meter-high mud walls. Of course, I take some photos of the construction sites to have a comparison from today to the pictures of 2011.

Ursula finds the path ugly at the beginning, but since the Carretera stretches far into the valley, it also has its beauty. I enjoy the path anyway because it is easy to walk. We, along with Luis, are the first pilgrims to arrive in Lubián. The hostel is a small stone house, and it is located in the lower part of the village. We lay out our sleeping bags to make sure, this bed is taken and go back outside. We can both remember that in the upper village, there is a bar that serves meals. And again, our brain still works fine. We have lunch there.

As we return, many pilgrims have arrived and by 4 p.m. all beds of the hostel are occupied.

After the siesta, Ursula and I walk back along the original path in opposite direction, as we want to know how much of the original and extremely beautiful path through the lush green landscape is still passable. But at some point, we turn back, as we no longer see any signs indicating possible blastings.

I hope that in a few years I can once again walk this path on the original route.

47 Lubián - A Gudiña

A beautiful morning gives rise to anticipation for today's stage. The Italians and Spaniards have already left at 6 a.m. We eat our poor breakfast (a yogurt and a banana) and a little later we also start walking. Three highlights are awaiting us for today. First, the crossing of the A Canda pass (1'260 MüM) which in my memory is a most beautiful walk and second, today we enter the autonomous region of Galicia (not to be confused with Galizia, which is in Poland). Thirdly, today we reach the 1'000 km mark.

But first, back to the path. First, we descend into the valley until we reach the Santuário de la Tuiza, which is dedicated to the 'Virgen de las Nieves' (Snow Maiden).

We then start the ascent on that beautiful natural path to the A Canda pass. I remember this part very well, but today it is even more beautiful, as the path is entirely lined with flowering broom and heather bushes. In two hours, we are at the top and by reaching the A Canda Pass we now enter Galicia.

The first Camino de Santiago way marker in Galicia stands on the A Canda pass and shows us the way ahead. These special way markers were created from sandstone by a Galician artist They will accompany us all the way to Santiago de Compostela.

The rest of the way is as beautiful as the ascent. The weather is beautiful and mild, the flowers and bushes shine in most intense colors. It is a comfortable pilgrimage in a magnificent landscape.

Vilavella, a small village down the valley has now a new bar and there we allow ourselves the first coffee of the day. Further the path leads on dirt roads, over stone bridges and hills, steadily downhill. Today I feel in top shape. At the small village of Pereira we reach the 1'000 km mark. This high point is only for Ursula and me, as we are currently the only pilgrims who have walked the Camino de Levante. We both have never walked this far in one piece. Antoine (a young Frenchman) is nearby and takes pictures of us.

Barely 25 km after the start we reach the hostel. In front of us, only the younger pilgrims have already arrived. For our age, this is a remarkable achievement.

Then follows the usual procedure for us. Eating, showering, washing, siesta, writing the travel diary, shopping, strolling around the village and scouting out the start of the route for tomorrow.

Galicia
Characteristic for Galicia are the high mountain ranges and the extremely green landscape, which reminds me of our Alpine foothill regions. Reading about Galicia in travel guides, it is always said that a lot of rain falls there. Except for the days in 2010, I was always spoiled with beautiful and warm weather. On most of the Caminos de Santiago the trails to Galicia cross mountains. These mountain crossings give me a feeling of joy and relief that I made it this far under my own power. In addition, there is the anticipation of the near goal of the pilgrimage in Santiago de Compostela.

Galicia and Switzerland

Galicia and I, we have a special connection. In 2010, when I was walking through the north of Galicia coming from the coastal path, I experienced a hospitality in a remote place that had to do with my nationality. I was walking with two German pilgrims. The weather was rainy and cold and in one stage place there was no restaurant nor store. However, the pilgrim hostel had a large and well-equipped kitchen and I decided to cock a typical Galician dish for my two fellow pilgrims and for myself. A 'Caldo Gallego' (stew with meat broth, potatoes, sausage and berzas). Berzas are green cabbage leaves that can be seen in all gardens in Galicia.

Thus, we walked to a farm nearby to buy ingredients for our meal. As we approached, the owner came out. He stood there wide legged in a dismissive attitude and asked what we wanted. I explained to him that I wanted to cook a Caldo Gallego and buy the ingredients from him. His brusque answer was - we have nothing!

I therefore asked him where I could buy some potatoes and berza leaves. Probably out of pure curiosity he asked me. Where are you from? Me: 'Suíza'. As if at that moment the sun had risen! He: "Suíza, oh, what a beautiful country! My brother has been living in Switzerland for years. You are very good to our people. In every place in Galicia lives at least one person who has worked in your country'.

I was perplexed, for me this was new. Needless to say, that from that moment on I could get everything I needed for the Caldo, including bone for a good broth. He also gave us eggs for a tortilla. He didn't want any money, but in wise foresight

I had packed enough smaller bills and unceremoniously put them in his shirt pocket.

According to my research, many Gallegos emigrated to Switzerland in the 60s/70s because they found too few opportunities to earn money in their country. Many returned to their village after retirement. However, many still live with us or still have family members in Switzerland. Since this encounter, I always enjoy coming back to Galicia.

48 A Gudiña - Campobecceros (Laza)

The weather forecast predicts again hot weather for the coming days and therefore we still start early in morning. I have been looking forward to today's stage for a long time. In good weather it is a dream route. It is easy walking and the views from the heights into the surrounding valleys and into the distant hill ranges is simply beautiful.

Although it has been said that the Camino is not greatly affected by the construction work on the AVE route, we can still feel it. In the past, a car would pass by on this panoramic route occasionally. Today it has a lot of traffic. In each car there are 1 to 4 construction workers in their green or yellow uniforms.

The path runs high along the large reservoir 'Embalse das Portas'. I really like such beautiful panoramic routes. To the north, on the other side of the reservoir, you can see mountains. When I look on Google Earth, I see that these are the mountains of the 'Parque Natural do Invernadeiro' (Natural Park).

Before Campobecceros the path crosses a hill with steep descent, and then the SHOCK!!! A huge construction site with a tunnel with two tubes for the AVE. I can understand the Galicians that they finally want to be connected with modern means to the rest of Spain and the capital Madrid. But I also understand the nature conservationists who do not want such cuts in nature. Difficult.

Around noon (after 21 km and with hot 29°C, or 84.2 °F) we reach Casa Nuñez at the edge of the village.

In 2011 we could sit there comfortably on the terrace to quench the great thirst and then take care of the rooms. Now, the terrace has become a winter garden and the tables are already dished up for 40 people. We quench our thirst with an Aquarius.

The pilgrimage guide says that half of the remaining route to Laza (another 11 km) is affected by access roads and transportation to the large construction site. It also says that due to these many workers there are no overnight accommodations available in Campobecceros. Consequently, we had already decided in advance against the 33 km stage and reserved places in a van.

The previously so beautiful stretch on a small natural road has now become an access road on which the big trucks drive back and forth incessantly. We are glad that we don't have to walk this. In Laza we spend the night in the modern, beautifully situated pilgrim hostel. Laza is a small village at 482 meters above sea level, with about 400 inhabitants. During the main pilgrimage season, about 30 pilgrims stay here every day. In the village itself there is a restaurant that caters to the needs of the pilgrims. There are daily menus for lunch and dinner, and for breakfast the owners open their restaurant already at 6:30 am.

Gradually, the pilgrims who have walked the whole way arrive. Their reports do not sound enthusiastic.

49 Laza - Vilar do Bario

After a quiet night we get up at 06 a.m. As usual, we first have breakfast and then move on.

It is simply beautiful. Although it is still cool, but after the first climb I can already take off my jacket. The second climb is much less steep than I remember. After three hours we are already at Luis and have a coffee. Luis is a former pilgrim who has converted his house in Alberguería into a pilgrims' meeting place. For this purpose, you can buy a shell and put your name and date on it. Luis will meticulously write it down in a big book and then hang it up in one of the rooms. When you come back here years later, he can tell you exactly where your shell is hanging. How many of them might be there in the meantime? It is clear that we personalize a shell again.

After half an hour we continue walking. Around noon we are already in Vilar do Bario, although it was again a 22 km stage over some hills.

From 12:30 the hostel opens, and we can move into the house and choose our beds. Afterwards we sit down on the small plaza and drink another water. Little by little, some pilgrims pass by, stay here, or decide to continue despite the heat.

On all Caminos there are always pilgrims who plan their pilgrimage very tightly and consequently cannot 'afford' half stages.

Cornelius (Holland) arrived alone because his friends had to abandon the Camino in Laza due to an acute inflammation. He will also spend the night here and now he joins us for lunch.

A slight cold is coming up, running nose and a slight sore throat. After the siesta, we go briefly to the tienda to shop. Then we sit down on the pretty plaza and watch the hustle and bustle. In Spain, towns and cities are almost deserted at siesta time. After 5 p.m., however, people come to the plaza from all sides. The adults meet for a drink, or an ice cream and the children romp around at the plaza. In contrast to our northern countries, people here enjoy this time outside very much.

50 Vilar do Barlo - Xunqueira de Ambía

It's full moon and we're in for another heat day. As no bar opens early for breakfast, we have provided for an Albergue breakfast, which is, yogurt, vending machine coffee and a bread roll.

The moon is still hanging on the sky as the three of us head out. Cornelius asked us last night if he could walk with us. These are always difficult decisions, since not all pilgrims make good companions. However, we have known Cornelius for 2 weeks and we both think that he is very handsome. Today's route is short with 13 km and also easy to walk. We keep crossing small villages or scattered settlements, most of which seem abandoned. In each village there are Horreos (granaries standing on granite supports). We know them from the many years on the road on the Caminos through Galicia.

At the last village before the rock crossing, I ask a man if there is a café nearby. He points to the nearby Carretera, where there is a bar. Since we started early, we decide to go the detour. For a good Café Solo (for me) or a Café con Leche (for Ursula) we gladly go two additional kilometers. Oh, almost forgot. Cornelius is walking with us now and he also drinks Café con Leche. By the way, the coffee is good!

Afterwards we walk back on the path and ascend to the picturesque rock crossing that everyone on this Camino remembers fondly. All pilgrims take photos of this section of the path in front of the rock formation.

Since we are already at the top at 10 o'clock, we sit down on the stone bench and enjoy the beautiful view of the wide surroundings.

Soon 2 bikers pass by who started in Villacañas (near Toledo), and today still ride to Ourense. Tomorrow Sunday, they want to reach Santiago. They are young and well trained, and will easily manage these remaining 100 km.

After the break, we continue and around noon we reach the hostel of Xunqueira de Ambía. The house is situated outside the village, and it is not very clean. I would have liked to stay in a nice Casa Rural, which I know from fall of 2011. But Ursula had already decided in advance for the hostel and as a pilgrim team you also must be able to compromise.

For lunch we go to the village. Afterwards back and siesta. In late afternoon we walk back to the village again and visit the church of the former monastery Colegiata de Santa María de Xunqueira de Ambía from the 12th century with the worth seeing cloister.
After the tour we sit down for a while on the plaza.

51 Xunqueira de Ambía - Ourense

Early in the morning it is foggy, a completely new experience for us. Today's stage is almost entirely on asphalt. Some sequences have remained in my memory, others less. It takes a good 2 hours until we find an open bar for a coffee. Because of the announced heat we don't allow ourselves long breaks and walk on. Soon we reach the industrial area of Ourense. On the street a bar advertises Huevos Fritos (fried eggs). I don't let myself be asked twice and Cornelius joins me. Ursula has something sweet with her coffee.

After being spoiled with stages in fantastically beautiful areas over the last few days, today's route feels a bit monotonous for me. But with the crossing of the picturesque village of Seixalbo with its massive stone houses, my mood immediately perks up again. This is followed by the descent into the valley basin of Ourense. This town is located in the river valley of the Río Miño at only 125 m above sea level and the expected temperature today is supposed to be 37°C / 98.6°F.

We arrive at the hostel already at 12 o'clock, but it opens only at 1 p.m. I sit down in the shade and take care of the backpacks, while Ursula and Cornelius visit the cloister of the monastery of San Francisco next door. At 1 p.m. we check in. I don't want to have lunch today but enjoy the atmosphere in the city in the evening hours and have some tapas. Perfect for all.

We stay in the house for a long siesta since we certainly can't go outside before 5 p.m. We start our evening tour with shopping for tomorrow. Afterwards we go down to the old town. The temperature gauge at the pharmacy still shows 37° at 6 p.m.

We visit the cathedral from the 12th and 13th century with the worth seeing main portal and get a pilgrim's stamp for our pilgrim's card. Then we enjoy an ice cream on the Plaza Mayor. We skip the visit to the Roman bridge for today, as we will cross it tomorrow on our way out of town.

If the temperature is as high as it is now, large white sun sails are hung over important squares and streets so that people can move around in the shade.

Later we sit down at one of the street bars, eat some tapas and drink a glass of Albariño (delicious Galician white Wine). This is how summer in the south feels like!

52 Ourense - Cea

Today is Sunday once again. The weather forecast predicts another hot day and therefore we leave after 6 a.m. It is a clear mild morning. Surprisingly, some bars are already open at this time. They open on Sunday morning to cater to the many young people on their way home. Although we have already had breakfast, we allow ourselves another coffee. Then we cross the beautiful Roman bridge over the Río Miño before beginning the steep ascent out of the valley basin.

The distance from Ourense to Santiago is a little over 100 km. There will be more pilgrims on is part, as many pilgrims walk only the last 100 km to Santiago de Compostela. This is the minimum distance to receive the Compostela, the document which promises the pilgrim indulgence from his sins.

In the various pilgrimage guides, three different variants are described for this stage. Ursula has previously gone the western way and still grumbles today about the arduous first 10 km on the shoulder of the busy road with a crisp slope. In 2011 we had decided to begin with the ascent on the eastern route, and in middle cross over to get to the western side. Unfortunately, we had not found the cross connection and had to go long kilometers along the road.

The 3rd option is the most beautiful, in my opinion. At the beginning the east variant, then a cross connection to the west and finally the rest of the way on the west variant. And that's what we want to walk today.

The eastern path climbs relatively steep up the surrounding hill range. From up there, 400 above sea level, there is a spectacular view of Ourense with its interesting bridges over the Río Miño. Passing by a group of houses above, we see many burned trees. A house owner tells us that a fire burned here last August. I often see such forest fires on TV, however, to see the effects in reality is impressive and somehow scary.

We follow the path until we reach a road junction, which we assume is the turnoff to Liñares. However, as in 2011, neither Liñares nor Cea is indicated on the road signs.

According to the position of the sun this junction looks correct, i.e., from east to west. In a hamlet we ask again, but once again the residents know nothing about the existing pilgrimage routes. On the street signs it says again and again Amoeiro and this is not in our pilgrimage guide. Suddenly we reach a small, scattered settlement and it is Liñares! We also see again the familiar arrows and way stones.

This beautiful trail put us in a high-spirited mood of adventure. A picnic area in the shade of the trees invites us to take a break. Then suddenly we are in front of the small original pilgrim station of César. A former pilgrim invites us for a drink and some cookies. He is happy to share with us his memories of previous journeys. After a short rest we must move on, as we have 10km left. Again, we walk on beautiful forest and field paths until we reach the old stone bridge of Ponte Mandrás. At a bar we stop again for a drink. I drink a 5 dl Aquarius bottle ex and fill up my drinking supply with another bottle. After another 5 km on beautiful trails through forests we reach Cea.

Even before we reach the village center, we see large posters advertising the wood-fired bread of Cea.

We will spend the night in the pilgrim hostel. Upon arrival we choose our beds and then go directly for lunch. Instead of the usual bread made from white flour, today we will get the specialty - wood oven bread from Cea.

After that follows our usual procedure: shower, wash, siesta. After 4 p.m. a Hospitalero comes by, and we can officially check in. Afterwards we go shopping and enjoy the mild evening hours on the plaza.

The hostel is almost completely occupied. We know the fewest pilgrims since many of them have started in Ourense and walk only the last 100 km from Ourense to Santiago.

53 Cea - Castro Dozón

On the main road of Cea there is a new bar that offers breakfast for pilgrims early in the morning. These are the amenities on much traveled paths. After breakfast we start walking.

From Cea there are again two options. A direct one, with long sections on the road, and a detour via the Cistercian monastery of Oseira. On this variant are many passages on natural paths. We choose the way via Oseira.

A fantastically beautiful trail awaits us. As yesterday, it is almost exclusively trails through forests, past old stone walls and meadows that spread a mystical atmosphere with their morning dew. Steadily, but moderately, we overcome the difference in altitude. We walk the whole way without seeing a single person and suddenly stand in front of this imposing monastery, which stands in absolute solitude.

It is shortly after 9 o'clock, but the monastery can only be visited from 10 o'clock and the tour would take an hour. Ursula has visited the monastery in 2009, I don't want to overexert my foot and Cornelius wants to continue. We decide to continue, but only after a coffee at the small bar next to the monastery. Then we tackle the long steep climb behind the monastery.

From above we can see the size of the Monastery. It always amazes me that in earlier times such large buildings could be built at all in this remoteness.

But then, the climb up the old stone path requires all our attention. At the top we sit down on stone walls in the shade and eat our picnic. Afterwards the trail continuous for about 3 hours, alternately up and downhill. The views keep changing and due to the clear air, we can see very far.

Along the way we pass small hamlets. Then suddenly we see a broken wooden sign 'BAR'. Through a cross connection we reach a simple bar with an inviting terrace and have a drink.

We continue walking through areas with agriculture. In some distance we see again and again zones with high eucalyptus trees. Galicia and northern Portugal started to plant these trees a long time ago. They grow very fast, and the wood is used for the paper industry. Unfortunately, at that time they didn't know that these trees displace all other plants in the area and only fern can prevail. In addition, these trees need a lot of water, and they also burn very quickly. This partly explains the huge forest fires that have occurred in recent years.

Then suddenly we reach the N-525 national road Ourense - Santiago. From here we walk the remaining kilometers to Castro Dozón. The pilgrim hostel is newly built, practically on the same place as before, but much nicer and airier. My bed is next to a window, and I can see the starry sky out of my sleeping bag.

At the hostel we are ten pilgrims. Among them is a young Canadian with severe tendinitis in his knee. He can no longer continue. In absence of a direct bus connection to Santiago, he must return to Ourense tomorrow, to take the direct bus from there to Santiago. He is very disappointed; this is not how he had imagined arriving in Santiago. I tell him about several pilgrims who had to break off their pilgrimage this way, but then walked the missing distance the following year. When you have a perspective, such a situation is suddenly not that bad.

54 Castro Dozón - Laxe

During the early morning hours, the wind has freshened up strongly. We get up at 05:40, eat a meager albergue breakfast and head out. I cannot remember today's stage. Let's see what awaits me. First, we walk for an hour along the Carretera, which is almost not used anymore since the highway is finished. On the left side of the road is a large restaurant, that unfortunately opens only at lunchtime. The morning atmosphere is incredibly beautiful. Again and again, we stop and take pictures of the spectacular sunrise.

Beautiful forest paths and a constant up and down follows. Then we cross the highway and from there I suddenly remember the route. After three hours we reach the village of Estación Lalin. Coming steeply out of the forest, we are 'spit out' onto a road. On the left-hand side is a big traffic circle and right next to it are a couple of restaurants offering fried eggs. What might we order?

After that break we follow a steep climb and then continuing on shady forest and beautiful field paths. Another unexpected change, and out of a shady forest path, we reach the highway and Carretera Junction and walk for another kilometer to the Albergue. At 12 o'clock we are there, but it opens only at 1 p.m. We wait in the shade on a bench. Check in, get our bed, and then go for lunch to a nearby bar.

Cornelius is now walking with us for the 6th day, and he seems to be very comfortable. He is a good walker, a pleasant pilgrim buddy and in addition also a funny and cheerful person. In meantime, he also knows that there is no need to get hungry with us, because we always find a restaurant with typical local meals. For a big lean man who likes to eat a lot, sandwiches are not optimal as food during a long pilgrimage.

Nutrition on the Caminos

In meantime, the readers of this book know our eating habits. We pay attention to a balanced nutrition and eat exclusively in local restaurants. Of course, we always have some provisions with us, which for me are preferably almonds and dried apricots or cranberries.

Many pilgrims cook their own food in the hostels and eat mainly pasta and sausages. From my point of view, not an optimal choice. I know in meantime that pilgrims who do not speak Spanish are overwhelmed by the choice of menus. My advice therefore goes to future Santiago pilgrims, learn Spanish in advance or have Spaniards write down a selection of dishes so that they do not have to eat the same food for 6 weeks.

55 Laxe - Bandeira

We really feel privileged, the weather forecast continues to promise beautiful weather and over 30°C (86°F). Because the bar in Laxe opens only at 8 o'clock for breakfast, we have decided yesterday evening again for a small Albergue breakfast and leave already at 06.30 o'clock. This time management will help us to reach Bandeira before the big heat.

As yesterday and the day before, it is a constant up and down on very beautiful paths. Galicia is very green everywhere thanks to the lush vegetation. After two hours we arrive at the Roman bridge that crosses the River Deza. After that, the trail leads on Roman cobblestones up and out of the valley to the N-525. However, only after some minutes, the trail branches off again and leads away from the road into the shady woods.

Soon the first place 'Silleda' follows, where we take time for a coffee and something sweet. From Silleda the routing triggers no enthusiasm with me. The way leads along the Carretera. But if there is a house directly by the road, the path leads down the slope, across any back alley, and then climbs back up to the road.

Because of this routing I decide for the road variant. Cornelius also comes along. On a steady pace we walk the remaining 8 km on the side strip of the busy road. At some point we see the white houses of Bandeira and calculate that we will be there around noon.

After arrival we sit down on the shady terrace of the hostal and wait for Ursula. As suspected, she arrives 15 minutes later. Check in, have lunch and siesta. Bandeira is a long village on the busy N-525 and offers nothing exciting.

I use the free afternoon hours to wash my hair and care for my hands and feet. Also, I wash all my laundry because it dries very quickly in this heat.

Tomorrow will be our second to last day on this Camino. This gives me the opportunity to reflect on the past two months. Ursula and I always make a game out of listing the stages and reviewing special experiences. Like singing Amapolas, staying in Toledo, dodging sprinklers, watching rabbits, photographing birds, eating in Puebla de Sanabria, etc.

56 Bandeira - A Vedra

In the morning it is hazy, and the humidity is very high. After a good breakfast we start. The way leads on small roads and through forests, fields, and past hamlets with the typical stone houses. In one village a stone house is being restored. This reminds me of Klosters, when large stone blocks were also used to renew the walls of the river Landquart.

After 3 hours we reach the mountain crossing near 'Ponte Ulla'. The view is impressive. A wide valley stretches before us, and two imposing bridges span the valley and the river. The smaller one is the railroad bridge of the line Ourense - Santiago. The big one was built for the AVE. When Ursula passed through here in 2009, the new railroad bridge was still under construction. When my sister and I passed through in 2011, it was finished but not yet in operation. Now the AVE already passes over it.

After we have taken enough pictures, we descend steeply and cross the old stone bridge to Ponte Ulla. At the end of the bridge is the restaurant Rios, which awaits us with delicious tostada and huevos fritos.

After this snack, the path climbs again from the river valley and around noon we are up in A Vedra, a scattered settlement where the pilgrim hostel of the Xunta de Galicia (Galician Provincial Government) is located. It opens around 1 p.m. The Hospitalera is still the same as in 2011. Friendly and competent. We choose our beds and inquire about the restaurant, which is a little further down in middle of the vineyards. Unfortunately, it has been closed for 2 years.

But the Hospitalera has an alternative ready for us pilgrims. She offers 'food to order', which we gladly accept. Our order looks like for a large family: 3 x mixed salad, 3 x fried eggs with chorizo, 3 x bread, 1 bottle of Albariño, 3 large bottles of water, and as dessert 3 x cheese with Membrillo (quince paste). Coffee is available from the vending machine. In addition, we order 3 bocadillo and 3 yogurts for tomorrow's breakfast. All together the costs are only 67 €. For me it is huge portions but fortunately Cornelius has a bigger appetite than me and there will be no leftovers.

57 A Vedra - Santiago de Compostela

It is Friday, June 20. The weather report on TV predicts a change in the weather for the weekend. My weather app, WeatherPro, which I've used for years, predicts thunderstorms with rain showers starting at 5p.m. Early morning is cloudy and hazy. The humidity is 89% and I can soon take off my jacket.

First, the path leads through a long forest, then again on small roads past hamlets and beautiful individual houses. These properties and houses show the proximity to a city.

Shortly before 8 o'clock we see a restaurant in front of us, but its shutters are closed. But as if someone had heard our coffee prayers, one store after the other opens. And when we cross the street, the door is also opened. Perfect. Considering our goal today. we don't linger long and set off again. The path leads over hills, up and down. At the lowest point, by a stream, stands a chapel.

The last climb up from the valley. Soon the path leads over a bridge of the AVE line, where the terrible train accident happened a year ago. On the bridge railings still hang photos and greeting messages.

A large handwritten poster reads: 47 Muertos, 46 Heridos, 0 Culpable. (47 Dead, 46 Injured, 0 Responsible). This affects me very much. Cornelius weeps quietly. It takes some time for us to get our emotions under control.

At 10:30 we arrive in Santiago. Like all other pilgrims, we first go to the large square in front of the cathedral, the Praza do Obradoiro. This is where all the Caminos de Santiago routes meet. I first enjoy this feeling of having arrived. Standing on this square is highly emotional for every Santiago pilgrim.

People spontaneously hug each other, and most are overjoyed. But there are always pilgrims who cry out of exhaustion or other feelings. It is not uncommon to meet fellow pilgrims who have not been seen for days or weeks.

Ursula and I have arrived in Santiago many times before, and still this arrival is special for us as well.

For Cornelius it is the first time, and he is overjoyed to have reached his goal after these long 1'000 km on the Via de la Plata.

At the former pilgrims' office next to the cathedral, the pilgrims who have arrived are already queuing up. We hope that most of them will go to the pilgrim mass at 12 o'clock and thus we first sit down in a bar for a drink. But we thought wrong. After noon, the queue has become a little shorter, but we must wait for a good hour to receive the Compostela (pilgrim's certificate).

Afterwards we go directly to lunch.

After lunch we go to our booked hotel. In the evening the three of us meet again and attend the evening mass at the cathedral.

Camino de Santiago / Way of St. James
Before Ursula and I set off tomorrow on the onward Camino from Santiago to Fisterra, I'm taking some time to write down my thoughts on pilgrimage in more detail.

What is the Way of St. James? The Way of St. James is a pilgrimage route that has as destination the alleged tomb of the Apostle James at the Cathedral of Santiago de Compostela.

Why do hundreds of thousands of people set out on the Way of St. James every year? People of all ages, all origins, and all nationalities?

Is it because there is a fascination with this path?
Is it the belief in a higher power?
Is it to start a new phase of life?
Is it to process a goodbye?
Is it to explore new territory?
Is it to focus on essentials?
Is it to be part of the pilgrimage movement?

These questions, which can also be found on the back of my book, represent only a small selection of the possible reasons. For me, the 3rd question, the new stage of life, was the decisive reason. After more than 4 4years of working life, mostly in rigid structures, the possibility to just leave and try something completely new was exactly what I wanted to do. To explore unknown areas of Spain on foot. To walk one of the Caminos de Santiago and be part of the pilgrim community. Meet other pilgrims and have a common path with them. In retrospect, it was the perfect start to my retired life.

Requirements for body and soul on the Way of St. James
So far in this book I have written little about the demands on our bodies and souls on the Camino de Santiago.

The body - what does it need?
Training, fitness, well broken-in shoes, a backpack that fits perfectly and is not too heavy (max. 10% of your own body weight), comfortable clothing (functional clothing is best because it is very light and dries quickly), rain jacket, rain pants and a sleeping bag.

The optimal training is not easy to define. At home, at least a month before departure, you should start walking every day with a backpack to get your shoulders used to the weight. But no one walks 5-6 hours every day for a month as a workout. Most think the training comes with the Camino.

I think that can be ok, BUT only, if the stages, especially in the beginning are not too long, and that you also schedule rest days. This helps to survive the exhaustion phases well and to give the body time to recover. For me, since the beginning my Camino stages are around 20 to 25 km long. Very important for me are also the rest days, which allow me to even walk long Caminos without problems.

The soul - what does it need?

I find that a difficult question. Very personal and emotional. On a pilgrimage, you meet many people. There are pilgrims who make it clear from the beginning that they want to walk alone. For me, that's okay. But there are also those who simply attach themselves to you and immediately start talking for hours. For me, that's rather not ok.

From my experience, many people have a good sense of whether you are on the same 'wavelength'. In any case, on my many Caminos I have met great people. People who have become friends in meantime and whom I would never have met without a Camino.

My soul only needs what the Camino gives me. It feels good to give space to the thoughts. It is like meditative walking over a long period of time.

↑ Cereal fields in Tierra del Pan/Bridge over Río Esla

↑ High above the Río Esla / Faramontanos de Tábara ↓

↑ Looking back / Encounters on the Camino ↓

Santiago Peregrino
The oldest known representation of a pilgrim St. James
(11th c.)
on the south portal of the Romanesque church of
Santa Croya de Tera

↑Descent from A Ganda Pass/ 1'000 km mark reached↓

↑ Panoramic path above the 'Das Portas' reservoir

↑ Dream path to the Rock passage / and rest ↓

↑ Ourense with the Río Miño / Oseira Monastery ↓

↑ Santiago in sight / The goal reached ↓

PART THREE

SANTIAGO - FINISTERRE

58 Santiago de Compostela - Negreira

Yesterday we arrived in Santiago. Normally, after arriving, we stay at least one more day in Santiago to enjoy this special atmosphere. But for this time, we decided in advance to continue already the following day towards Finisterre (Fisterra) to finish our project.

During the night it rained heavily, but in the morning, it is dry and from our room we can see the beautiful morning atmosphere. Breakfast is served from 07:30. Cornelius also comes down to say goodbye. He will meet later with his wife, who will arrive today by plane in Santiago.

Ursula and I start walking again. The weather is much nicer than announced. The stage begins beautifully, because it leads immediately out of the town of Santiago and onto the way in the wilderness. After a short time, there is a stone figure of St. James at a house with an 'azulejo' (tile) on which the request 'Ánimo' (head up!) is written. Even if the 'Camino de Fisterra' is only 100 km long, I like such encouragement.

The stage is easy to walk, although there are two altos (mountain crossings) to pass. After the first alto, there is a large restaurant at a road crossing and all pilgrims take a break here.

There are really many pilgrims on the way, as Carlos (a Hospitalero from Zamora) announced. Many young people from the Camino Francés, a large group of Portuguese and many Italians.

The way leads for long passages through eucalyptus forests. These forests smell good but despite the smell, for me they are like dead forests. You don't hear birds chirping nor do you see rabbits.

After a few hours we reach Ponte Maceira. A small town on the way, with a beautiful Roman bridge. We take our time for some pictures and then walk through to Negreira.

Because we only left at 08:30, its already 2 p.m. until we arrive in Negreira. We walk to the private hostel San José and as usual, we are welcomed very friendly. The first time I stayed in this hostel, a young woman screamed out loud with joy when she saw my ID. 'Oh, you are from Switzerland and from the canton of Grisons'. As it turned out, she had grown up as the child of Galician emigrants in Chur, Switzerland. Now she has returned to Galicia with her husband.

Afterwards we go to have lunch at the restaurant O Noso Lar, a tip from the hostel. There are only locals here and the food is excellent. At the hostel, we briefly met Benito, a pilgrim we have known for a long time. He will also eat at the same restaurant.

In the afternoon follow again our pilgrim duties. Siesta, shower, washing. Then shopping and go in search of a bar for breakfast tomorrow. Afterwards we sit outside at a bar in the sunshine. There are still many pilgrims passing by who want to spend the night in the hostel of the parish. This hostel is located outside Negreira.

59 Negreira - Olveiroa

In the morning, surprisingly, there is dense fog. We have breakfast at the nearby bar. After that we start walking. It soon clears up and again it is beautiful weather. The paths are pleasant to walk. There are lot of pilgrims on the way, but that doesn't bother us, as everyone seems to be happy. After about 3 hours, in Vilaserio, a bar is open, and we take a coffee break. Then we walk on. At a hill there are nice views and photo subjects. After that, the path leads steadily downhill.

In Santa Mariña (after 22 km) there is a cab waiting. We have not ordered one, even though we do not want to walk the remaining 10 km from here. But the cab first takes three men to Olveiroa and then comes back. While we wait, we drink something and talk with the other pilgrims. When the cab is back it takes us to Casa Loncho in Olveiroa. The private rooms at the hostal are unfortunately fully booked, therefore we sleep for the last time on this Camino in the dormitory. After 4 p-m-we sit on the terrace of the bar, and it starts to rain. Still, many pilgrims pass by who have walked the whole 32 km. Meanwhile, the dormitory is also fully booked. In the village there is another hostel of the municipality and in 6 km distance there is another private hostel. When exhausted pilgrims ask for a bed at the bar, and Olveiroa is fully booked, it can happen, that the owner drives them to the hostel which is located km 6 away.

Olveiroa is a small town (about 120 inhabitants), which is a staging post on the extended pilgrimage route from Santiago to Finisterre.

The private hostel 'Casa Loncho' is a family business where all family members collaborate. Competent and friendly.

Later in the afternoon, the restaurant is fully occupied because all the pilgrims, about 60 in number, want to eat here. I am amazed at how well the service works, although only a few pilgrims speak Spanish.

60 Olveiroa - Fisterra

In the morning it is very cloudy, and we even consider putting on the rain pants. But then we decide otherwise and still go without. It is a mystical atmosphere and there are many pilgrims on the way. The path climbs quickly in direction of the windmills, but then turns onto a panoramic path. On the left below is a reservoir. From Hospital the path splits. On the left, it leads towards the sea and over Cee and Corcubión to Fisterra. The right fork continues to Muxía via Dumbria.

We have chosen the left, direct variant to Fisterra. Soon it becomes brighter, still windy, but visibly sunnier. As soon as we can see the sea and in distance Cap Finisterre, we stop for photo sessions. On the way we meet pilgrims who also walk the same stage as we do.

In Cee, a larger town on a sea bay, we stop for a short coffee stop, and then continue walking along the Paseo Maritimo. At the end of the bay, in Corcubión, there is a restaurant where we want to have lunch It is 1 p.m. and we must wait 10 minutes until they serve food. As appetizer a vegetable platter that would have been good for 3 - 4 people. The main course is Ternera en salsa (roast beef in sauce).

Shortly after the appetizer, the main course follows. A large plate is put in front of me, on which are about 6 slices of roast. It is a lot, but we think that it will be for both of us. Wrong thought! Ursula also receives such a plate. We return one of them immediately and still don't manage to eat the whole portion for two.

After 2 p.m we walk on. First comes the climb to San Roque, which, contrary to the description in the pilgrimage guide, I don't find it extremely steep. After crossing the range of hills, the road lowers again and we come to the nice beach villages of Estorde and Sardiñeiro. After these two villages, the road follows the coast. On the left the sea, shining in most beautiful shades of blue and turquoise, on the right the range of hills shines in intense broom yellow.

We are heading towards our final destination Fisterra.

The weather has changed slowly, and it seems that a thunderstorm is coming up. We hurry to arrive in Fisterra before the thunderstorm. Arrival at the booked hostal at 3 p.m. I feel exhausted and know exactly, why I normally avoid such long stages.

A R R I V E D   L L E G A D O

What a feeling! We have really made it.
1,300 km on foot across Spain. We would love to shout it out very loud and tell the whole world.

But for now, we just enjoy it.

↑Pilgrims on Plaza Obradoiro/Cathedral of Santiago ↓

Statue of St. James on the way to Finisterre

↑ Ponte Maceira / Hórreo (Grain silo) ↓

↑ On the way from Negreira to Olveiroa ↓

↑ Pilgrims just before Cee / View of Corcubión ↓

↑With bare feet in the Atlantic/Cabo Finisterre km 0 ↓

61 Rest Day in Finisterre

Our hostal is located directly at the harbor of Fisterra. The seagulls are screeching loudly, it is sunny, and it smells of the sea. We have been to Fisterra many times and feel at home here. For breakfast we go to the Bar Frontera, across from our hostal. We greet the owners, whom we have known for a long time, of course, and enjoy sitting on the terrace by the harbor.

What more do I want? I am just happy!
This I could probably write in 'we' form.
What more do we want? We are just happy!

After breakfast, we walk the remaining 4 km to Cap Finisterre, where the 0 km milestone is located. Looking out to sea, chatting with other pilgrims, watching emerald lizards. Just let the soul dangle.

Then we slowly make our way back to Fisterra for lunch and siesta before heading to Langosteira Beach. We still want to fulfill our motto 'Dal Mediterráneo al Atlantico'. Stand with bare feet in the Atlantic Sea, beaming. unbelievable!

And now?

I am already starting to miss my Camino!